Law Soup Media presents:

Law is Not for Lawyers
(It's for Everyone)

Empower Yourself with the Basics of Law and Civics

Tristan Blaine, Esq.

Published by:
Law Soup Media

Copyright © 2023 by Tristan Blaine

All rights reserved. No part of this book may be reproduced or transmitted in any form or by any means, without written permission from the publisher.

Law Soup Media is owned by Tristan Blaine via a benefit corporation, The Enlightenment Co. Law Soup and Law Soup Media are claimed trademarks of Tristan Blaine.

2nd Edition. First trade paperback edition published 2019. Printed in the United States of America, using paper not sourced from endangered old growth forests, forests of exceptional conservation value, or the Amazon Basin.

ISBN 979-8-218-18583-1

About the Author

Tristan Blaine founded Law Soup Media in 2014 and currently serves as its Editor-in-Chief. As a California-licensed lawyer, he helps people start and grow businesses of all kinds, with a focus on social enterprise (B Corps/benefit corporations).

Recognized as a leader in the community, he has been selected to the Super Lawyers list for several years. He has written articles for Forbes.com and other publications. Tristan volunteers with the Los Angeles LGBT Center, and has secured asylum for LGBT victims of persecution.

He received his bachelor's degree from UCLA, and obtained a law degree, with a concentration in Constitutional Law and Rights, from Cardozo Law School in New York City. Tristan enjoys meditation, yoga, and hiking in the mountains of Southern California.

About Law Soup Media

The Laws You Need to Know. In Edible Form.

Law Soup Media explains the law, simply. We tell you what you need to know about your legal rights and duties, civics and our government, and how it all works (or doesn't). This information empowers you to take charge of your life and to make a positive impact on society. Law Soup Media provides this content through a variety of media, including books, free web content, an app, and a chatbot.

Law Soup Media's *Law is for Everyone* series

Law is Not for Lawyers (It's for Everyone):
 Empower Yourself with the Basics of Law and Civics

How to Be Free(lance):
 What Every Self-Employed Person Needs to Know About Law and Taxes

Do it Like a Boss:
 What Every Small Business Owner Needs to Know About Law and Taxes

Overview

Preamble: Why I Wrote this Book, and How to Get the Most Out of it

Article 1: How Did We Get Here?

Article 2: How Does the Legal and Government System Work (and Not Work)?

Article 3: What Rights (and Duties) Do I Have?

Article 4: How Do I Exercise My Rights (and Fulfill My Duties)?

Article 5: Where Do We Go from Here?

Appendices:
Legalese Translator (Glossary of Common Legal Terms)
References

Contents

Preamble: Why I Wrote this Book, and How to Get the Most Out of it 1

   A Bit About Me 5
   A Few Important Things to Note 7

      This is Not Legal Advice 7
      Exceptions to the Rule 7
      Gray Areas 8
      Everything Changes 8
      Facts vs Opinions 9
      Nobody's Perfect 9

   How to Use this Book 9

   Article 1: How Did We Get Here? 11

   Section 1: A Law is Born 13
   Section 2: How Did We Get Our Government and Legal System? 15

      Early Justice 15
      Law as King 17
      America: Heck Ya 19

   Section 3: How Strong Should Government Be? 21

      Law & Order (IRL) 21

What Do People Want from Government? 22

Section 4: How Did We Get So Many Laws? 25

See, the Problem is... 25
How it Got So Bad 28
A Modest Proposal: Culture as Cure............................ 33

Section 5: How Did We Get Here: A Recap 35

Article 2: How Does the Legal and Government System Work (or Not Work)?...37

What are the Levels of Government?........................... 39

Section 1: Who's in Charge Here?..40

Law is King 40
What is a Law, Anyway? 44

Section 2: Who Makes the Rules Around Here?.......... 45

1. Legislative Bodies – Makin' the Law 45
2. Executive as Lawmaker Lite.. 49
3. Courts Play Lawmaker, Too..50
4. Founders of Country or State – the OGs...............50
5. Voters – Yes, That's You 50
6. Parties to a Contract: A Private Show.......................51

Section 3: Who Enforces the Rules Around Here? 51

1. Executive: Enforcer-in-Chief 52
2. Legislatures as Enforcer... 58

   3. Courts as Enforcer 58

Section 4: Who Says What the Law is? 60

   1. Courts as Interpreters of Law 60
   2. Executive as Interpreter of Law 68

Section 5: Whose Law is it, Anyway? 68
Section 6: How Does it All Affect Me? 81

   Actions Have Consequences 81
   Where Am I? (Jurisdictionally Speaking) 85
   Illegal Laws 87
   It's All a Process 90
   How Appealing 97

Section 7: Let's Get Real 100

Article 3: What Rights (and Duties) Do I Have? 105

Section 1: What are My Civil Rights? 108

   Free Speech and Expression 108
   Religious Rights 108
   Rights Against Law Enforcement Overreach 109
   "Innocent Until Proven Guilty" 109
   No Cruel and Unusual Punishment 110
   Who Gets to Be a Citizen? 110
   Who Gets to Vote? 111
   Equality & Discrimination 111
   Reproductive Rights 114

Right to Own Guns for Self-defense..............................115

Section 2: What are My Rights in Interacting with the Police?..115

Due Process & the Police..116
Confrontations with Police... 117
Searches 118
Seizures: When can the police take my property?
.... 120
Arrests..121
Excessive Force 124
Lying to Police..125

Section 3: What are My Rights If I Am a Victim of Crime? 125

Law Enforcement Duty to Investigate Crime and Protect Victims..126
Victims' Rights Before Criminal Charges Filed......126
Victims' Rights After Charges Filed.............................127
Hate Crimes..128
Deadlines for Prosecuting Assailant............................128

Section 4: What are My Free Speech Rights? 128

Protected Speech 129
Unprotected Speech 132
Compelled Speech 133

Free Speech & Private Actors (Non-Government) 134

Section 5: What are My Privacy Rights? 135

    What is Considered an Invasion of Privacy? 135
    Personal Space 135
    Your Private Information & Data 136
    Rights in Your Identity 138
    Mail, Email and other Communications 140

Section 6: What are My Rights in My Home? 140

    Trespass & Disturbances 140
    Regulation of Property Ownership 141
    Renters Rights 143

Section 7: What Do I Need to Know About Contracts? 144

    What is a Contract? 144
    Enforceability 146
    Getting Out 147
    In Breach 148

Article 4: How Do I Exercise My Rights (and Fulfill My Duties)? 151

    Section 1: Options for Legal Help 154
    Section 2: How Do I Get and Work with a Lawyer? .. 157
    Section 3: Putting Government to Work 161

- Exercising Agency with Agencies 161
- Pressing Charges 162
- Section 4: Apps & DIY Legal 163
  - Non-lawyer Legal Services 163
  - DIY Legal Research 164
- Article 5: Where Do We Go from Here? 167
  - What Do We Know? 169
  - Towards a Stronger Civic Culture 172
  - What Are We Going to Do Now? 173
  - Acknowledgments 176
  - Legalese Translator: Glossary of Common Legal Terms 177
    - Symbols & Abbreviations 184
    - References 186

Preamble:
Why I Wrote this Book, and How to Get the Most Out of it

Preamble: Why I Wrote this Book, and How to Get the Most Out of it

You may be surprised that a lawyer is saying that Law is Not for Lawyers. I'm not saying we don't need lawyers. But the law affects all people, and everyone needs to know about the law and the legal system.

Knowing the law can significantly improve the quality of your everyday life. Consider some typical scenarios:

1. Your boss says she found out about your political activities and can't allow someone with your politics to work here. Can she fire you for that?

2. You get a notice that your landlord is doubling the rent next month. Can he do that?

3. You signed a contract yesterday for a contractor to renovate your kitchen. But now you realize you can't afford it right now. Do you have the right to get out of the contract?

Knowing the law in these situations could help you save your job (or get compensated for losing it), prevent your rent from increasing, or get out of an expensive contract. Clearly, there are measurable benefits to knowing the law. You could even say it's worth thousands of dollars per year.

As important as it is that we all understand the law, most of us don't even have the basics down. For example, can you answer the question: "What is the supreme law of the land?" The answer is on the next page, so take a moment to think about it (don't peek!)...

The highest law in the land is... the **U.S. Constitution**. If you knew that one, congratulations! You are one of the few, the select, the 30% of Americans who can answer this question.[1] If not, don't worry, you're not alone – you're in the 70%. And now that you know this one, you can join the 30%. Congratulations to you as well.

Here's another one that's just as important, but even fewer people know: The three branches of government. If you can name all three you are among only about ¼ of Americans![2] They are, of course, the **legislative, executive, and judicial**. This is not just an abstract or trivial fact. All three branches have a major influence on your life. You need to know who has the power to carry out the various functions of the system so that you can get what you need, exercise your rights, and call people out when they overstep their boundaries.

While most people had some form of civics class in school, these classes are often treated as an afterthought rather than as among the most important subjects. And very few of them focus on the legal system in particular. *Law is Not for Lawyers (It's for Everyone)* is in part a civics refresher, because you can't get a basic understanding of the legal system without understanding the governmental system. They are intertwined.

As beneficial as it is to know the law, it's also literally *required*. As crazy as it sounds, each one of us is expected to know all of the thousands of laws that apply to us at all times. Even if you have no idea you did something illegal, you can still face the penalties just the same.

Of course, in reality nobody can possibly know all of these laws, not even lawyers, judges, or police officers. And quite often, if you're really nice (or rich and powerful), maybe, just maybe, you can get off with only a warning. But maybe you aren't rich and powerful. Or nice. So, the more you know (cue the music and shooting star graphic), the better.

This book is your pocket guide (it really fits in your pocket!) to The System. A practical handbook to give you actionable information for your daily life. If knowledge is power, knowledge of the laws makes you quite powerful. I am able to exercise my rights, not because I am a lawyer (although that certainly helps), but mostly because I simply know the law. Ideally, everyone would get a full legal education. Of course, this is not practical. Here, you will learn some of the most important things I learned in law school and in my law practice, so you don't need to spend over $100K and many years to get up to speed.

A Bit About Me

In 2009, full of optimism and idealism, I went to law school to work towards that great promise of "liberty and justice for all." Yes, really! I received a concentration in constitutional law and rights, ready to make the world a little more fair for everyone. I figured most other lawyers were interested in the same. But I soon became disillusioned. After graduating and working for other lawyers, I realized there were not enough lawyers dedicated to providing high-quality legal services at reasonable rates.

So, in 2014 I started my own law practice to make legal services more accessible to small businesses. I focus on advising and teaching people how to make the law work for them, explaining it in a way that normal people can understand. I also believe in using simple, reasonable, transparent pricing. Unfortunately, this approach is all too rare. But it's the right thing to do.

Around the same time that I started my law practice, I also created Law Soup Media to provide free and low-cost legal information to the public about many areas of the law – from consumer issues, to employment, renters rights, civil rights, small business law, and much more. It started with a website, LawSoup.org, and now we have published these Law Soup Media books.

By purchasing the books, you are not only helping yourself, but you are also helping us with our mission to democratize the law and provide free online information, so thank you for that. You can further spread the love and knowledge by gifting the book to others. Thanks again!

A Few Important Things to Note

This is Not Legal Advice

Reading this book does not mean you can necessarily handle your own legal issues. It does not take the place of actual legal advice from an actual lawyer who can tell you how the law applies to your particular situation. Nothing in here is meant to be legal *advice*. Rather, it's general legal *information*. But, kind of like how real soup can help prevent health issues, *Law is Not for Lawyers* and the Law Soup website can help prevent legal issues.

You will almost certainly need a lawyer from time to time, and I will emphasize this at various times throughout (maybe too often!). The information here can help you be more confident and efficient in consulting with lawyers about your issues and concerns. It will save you money and time (and time is money, so you'll save *lots* of money).

Exceptions to the Rule

A law or legal principle that seems simple and straightforward may not always hold true in every situation. There are almost always exceptions to a rule. Life is messy, so law is messy.

When explaining a law or concept, I try to use terms like "generally" or "in general" to indicate that there are or may be exceptions. You will see these words frequently throughout.

Even when I don't use these terms, keep in mind there are always exceptions, except when there aren't. Just accept it.

Gray Areas

Related to the concept of exceptions to the rule is the idea that the law is filled with gray areas. (Or is it *grey* areas? This is its own gray area). While many legal rules or principles are firmly settled and generally free from doubt or dispute (known as **black letter law**), others may be ambiguous or in flux. I do my best to let you know how solid a rule is or isn't.

Even when a rule is settled, it may be a gray area as to whether the facts support a finding one way or another. An example is the requirement that a party to a contract must clearly indicate their agreement to that contract. What counts as indicating agreement may be up for interpretation.

How about if you propose a deal, and the other person responds "looks good," or simply "OK"? Did that person definitely agree to the terms of the contract, or were they merely acknowledging that they received it or reviewed it? Ultimately, this may need to be decided by a judge or jury.

Everything Changes

As with life, the law changes all the time, so some of the information here may be out of date at some point. Check the Law Soup website and discuss with a lawyer to make sure you have the latest info.

Facts vs Opinions

Alongside the straightforward facts about the law and the legal and government system, I often share my opinions about how things could be improved. I don't expect you to necessarily agree with me, and I encourage you to challenge me on my positions. My aim is to stimulate discussion about the issues, and to get you to think about things in a new way. Remember that the system is created by people, and we should not simply accept anything as the way it must always be. (There's an opinion already!)

Nobody's Perfect

Even with significant research and fact-checking (see the References section at the end), mistakes and inaccuracies are inevitable. Please help us and everyone else by letting us know if you think you see an error!

How to Use this Book

Law is Not for Lawyers is the first book in the *Law is for Everyone* series. After you read it, you may also want to read the others in the series that are specific to certain types of people, including freelancers, small business owners, etc.

You may be tempted to skip over some parts of the book which do not seem relevant to you at this particular time in your life. Maybe you think you will go back and read it later. But this is not the right approach.

First, you need to know the basics of the legal system *before* you have any issues, so that when an emergency or surprising event comes up, you won't worry so much because you will have a sense of how serious or not serious it is. And you will have a general idea how to start dealing with it. After you've read the book once, and later you have a question that you have forgotten the answer to, you can then come back and quickly scan through the table of contents and see if it's in here.

Secondly, everything is connected, and it starts to make much more sense when you learn how all the pieces fit together. This is why the historical and political parts are important.

But the most important reason to learn about all of this is for the good of society. The United States of America cannot work for the people if the people don't make it work. And it starts with understanding how it all works. It is your moral and legal duty to be informed. Here is your opportunity.

Happy reading!

Article 1:
How Did We Get Here?

Article 1: How Did We Get Here?

Well, first there was a big bang...but let's skip ahead a bit. To understand our current system of law and government in the United States, it's helpful to get a brief history of where it all came from.

Section 1: A Law is Born

Humans haven't always had government and legal systems. For thousands of years, as nomadic hunter-gatherer societies, and even horticultural societies, humans carried on without laws and without a formal government. Some of these still exist in certain isolated parts of the world.[3]

In fact, some such societal structures are even *less* formal than those of chimpanzees, one of humanity's two closest relatives. Chimpanzees typically organize into an extreme alpha-male hierarchy. The high-ranking members maintain the structure by carrying out violence against any challengers. Early human societies rejected this kind of centralized authority, instead favoring a highly egalitarian and cooperative system. Indeed, as many anthropologists argue, humans may have evolved away from chimpanzees in part due to a resistance to domination.[4]

This kind of "benign" or primitive anarchy simply doesn't hold up with larger and more complex environments. As people started developing larger scale agriculture and water control methods, around 11,000 years ago, this allowed for greater population density. And more people living near each other means one thing... neighbor disputes.

In order to help resolve these conflicts, certain people began to take it upon themselves to decide who was right and who was wrong. These decisions became "the law" and were enforced by these leaders and their associates. Gradually, these leaders established themselves in more permanent positions of power, with bureaucracies to carry out their decisions.

This process of the creation of government and legal systems has been compared to the formation of stars. Like stars, "cities and states reorganize and energize the smaller objects within their gravitational field."[5] In a new society, at a certain point the pressure of the interactions of so many people builds up. When the pressure becomes strong enough, new complex governmental structures are "forced" into existence to resolve problems and maintain a stable equilibrium.

Around 3000 BCE, humanity's first formal systems of law and government arose in the Middle East and Asia.[6] These systems were developed for the primary purpose of maintaining order and peace amidst increasing complexity. As humans have expanded over time and geography, such systems have developed into vehicles for ensuring fairness and equality, but also for purposes of oppressing and dominating others. These competing impulses are within us to this day, and likely always will be.

Particularly in a democracy, we, the people, have the choice as to the purpose of our laws and government. We must continually work to ensure that they are used for the good of others.

Section 2: How Did We Get Our Government and Legal System?

Early Justice

More than a thousand years after the first governments materialized, King Hammurabi of ancient Babylonia (present-day Iraq) created his now famous legal system. The Code of Hammurabi was one of the first justice systems to establish the concepts of **innocent until proven guilty**, and punishments proportionate to the severity of the crime.

While we can marvel at such an early example of a seemingly fair and just system, there were, of course, less positive aspects to the Hammurabi Code. Women and slaves were given worse treatment. And the principle of **an eye for an eye** meant perpetrators were punished in exactly the same way as the crimes they had committed. Although many people are still inclined to carry out this form of retribution, it is now generally regarded as counter-productive.

Over thousands of years and thousands of miles across the world, legal and political systems evolved into ever more enlightened societies which uphold individual rights. Many also devolved into utter chaos and **failed states**, at one extreme, and absolutist and totalitarian states on the other. Human history reflects a back and forth of the power of the people versus the consolidation of power into the hands of a few. Yet the overall trend has been towards an increase in our power.

"An eye for an eye leaves everyone blind."

– Coretta Scott King

Around 600 BCE, the Greeks developed the world's first known democracy. Soon after, the Roman Republic created a complex semi-democratic government which included the famous Roman Senate. As groundbreaking as it was to set up and maintain any form of democracy, still, these systems were not exactly inclusive. Interestingly, the word "senate" originates from the Latin word for "old man." Even today, despite a recent increase in the diversity of its members, our U.S. Senate is mostly a bunch of old (white) men![7]

Law as King

Unfortunately, these early attempts at participatory government collapsed as a result of ongoing fighting, both internal and external. Things got pretty dark for a while (yes, I'm talking about the Dark Ages) for human rights. But a bright spot appeared in 1215 when the aristocracy of England forced King John to sign a little piece of paper called the **Magna Carta** (the "Great Charter").

This revolutionary document ensured that even the King was not above the laws! It was essentially the first governing document to ever explicitly exert greater authority in the document itself than in a ruler.

When the laws rule the rulers, this is known, appropriately, as **Rule of Law**. It was a truly radical concept at the time (and oddly enough it is still somewhat controversial, even 800 years later). Before the Magna Carta, it was generally presumed that the rulers *decide* the rules, and thus don't have to necessarily *follow* the rules, because they could simply change them at any time.

Even democratic societies had generally held to the principle that they did not need to follow their own rules. Elected rulers argued that they were acting on behalf of the people, and thus had "proper" authority. But rule of law is just as important for democracies, because even democracies are capable of infringing on the rights of individuals. The fact that a majority of people may support this kind of infringement of rights doesn't make it OK.

Take one recent example. In 2008, a slim majority (52%) of California voters banned marriage equality for same-sex couples by voting for *Proposition 8*. Ultimately the courts ruled that Prop 8 violated the rule of law – specifically the law of the U.S. Constitution, which states that all people shall be treated equally under the law. Activists at the time said that #LoveWon, but actually, #RuleofLawWon.

Back to King John. He definitely did not like following any rules, and often took arbitrary and vindictive actions against even the most powerful people. In one extreme situation, he demanded an exorbitant sum of money from a powerful landowner in Ireland. When the landowner refused to pay, John imprisoned his wife and one of his sons, resulting in their deaths.[8] Understandably, the powerful elites were not happy with this situation, and they took matters into their own hands.

One of Magna Carta's most important provisions stated that the King could not arbitrarily arrest, imprison, or seize property from any "free man" without "the lawful judgment of his peers or by the law of the land."[9] This is an early version of **due process of law** (usually shortened as **due process**), which means the government must provide a fair and impartial procedure when enforcing the law.

If you get anything out of this book, let it be the two essential concepts of rule of law and due process. We will discuss these concepts much more in depth, so you will be able to understand them better.

America: Heck Ya

Cut to 1789, when the requisite number of American states ratified the new United States Constitution. The Constitution guaranteed that (and still does, at least as of this writing in 2022): "No person shall... be deprived of life, liberty, or property, without due process of law..." (5th Amendment) and "In all criminal prosecutions, the accused shall enjoy the right to a speedy and public trial, by an impartial jury of the state and district wherein the crime shall have been committed..." (6th Amendment). Does that sound similar to a certain document from 1215?

As we know, the American system did not live up to its elegant words at first (and we still have some work to do). Our founding document originally provided cover for slavery, declaring that slaves were to be counted as three-fifths of a person for purposes of counting population.

But the system continued to evolve, most dramatically during and after the Civil War, when slavery was finally abolished, and **equal protection of the laws** was enshrined in the Constitution (1868). Since then, the right to vote has been expanded to just about every adult U.S. citizen, including women in 1920. And the U.S. Supreme Court has expanded the interpretation of much of the Constitution such that we now have strong rights of freedom of speech, rights of privacy, and protection against law enforcement overreach.

> *"A prime part of the history of our Constitution is the story of the extension of constitutional rights to people once ignored or excluded."*
>
> *– Ruth Bader Ginsburg, Supreme Court Justice*

Still, in practice these rights are not always afforded to everyone. Laws and courts cannot make things happen on their own. It requires the people doing the daily work of the law – particularly police officers and government officials –

to internalize that every single person deserves these rights. We must hold these officials to the high standards we set in our governing documents.

Section 3: How Strong Should Government Be?

Law & Order (IRL)

As we have seen, laws and government were created to maintain order and peace. If the government isn't strong enough, the system can degenerate into utter chaos and a failed state. You might call this the "bad" kind of anarchy, or **state collapse anarchy**, as opposed to the **pre-state anarchy** of early humans. It usually involves widespread violence, theft, and extreme poverty. A failed state generally reflects a legal and government system which is powerless – or too complicit and corrupt – to do anything to improve the situation. [10] Examples include the brutal civil wars and genocides in countries like the former Yugoslavia, and over 30 countries today, such as Yemen and Somalia.[11]

On the other hand, too much "law and order" can be even worse. In authoritarian regimes such as Nazi Germany and the Soviet Union, the government could arrest and even execute individuals without needing to provide evidence of any legitimate crimes. In contrast, the United States system protects against this kind of tyranny with the principles of

rule of law and **due process**. Again, this means that the government is subject to certain rules, and may not deprive any person of life, liberty, or property without following proper, fair procedures.

Clearly, it's tricky to maintain a stable system with the right balance of power between the government and the people. Too little government power, and you may get chaos. On the other end of the spectrum, a regime that has *too much* power can be even worse than no government at all.

Laws, and particularly the rule of law, can help maintain this balance by putting up guardrails so government officials stay within the boundaries, while still empowering leaders to take necessary and appropriate actions to safeguard society. Yet laws alone can't stabilize and rein in the powerful. Attitudes promoting civic pride and limited government must be cultivated within the culture. These are nonpartisan ideals, but unfortunately, people on both the political Left and Right often fall short of these.

What Do People Want from Government?

Some people on the Left want a very strong government to ensure corporate interests don't overshadow the interests of the general public. A laudable goal, but instead of relying solely on government, society must also emphasize a culture of ethics and human-centered norms.

The Right is traditionally the most vehemently opposed to "big government." Despite this, many on the Right want to continue strengthening an already very powerful military and law enforcement system.

One thing many people on both the Left and Right agree on in using the power of government, unfortunately, is to censor speech that offends them. Of course, they generally don't agree on what particular content should be allowed and what should be blocked. So how could government officials even make the "right" decisions on this? For the most part, they can't, and they shouldn't. Free speech is too important and too complicated to regulate, aside from certain things like inciting violence, which we will discuss.

Almost nobody truly wants a large and complex government simply for the sake of having a large government. People across the political spectrum want to use this power as a means to serve their own desired ends. But once power is granted to the government, it's hard to take it back. Thus, we all have a responsibility to uphold universal civic values, and to call out leaders, even on our own "side," when they go too far.

Law and government are not inherently bad or inherently good, despite the claims of people throughout the political spectrum. Rather, it's what humans choose to do with the system that determines its power and purpose. Too much power in anyone's hands is a recipe for disaster.

Today, we have a large, complex system of law and government, with many laws, and much government. This is simply a fact. Is the system too large? Is the government simply not focusing on the right things? These are questions liberals and conservatives legitimately disagree about. But the fact is that we have large government bureaucracies (yes multiple bureaucracies – federal, state, and local), and many, many laws.

"Democracy is the worst form of government except for all those other forms that have been tried from time to time."

– Winston Churchill

Section 4: How Did We Get So Many Laws?
See, the Problem is...

There are thousands of laws in the U.S., including over 300,000 federal laws and regulations![12] And that's not even considering state and local laws. They keep coming too, with thousands more created each year.

In theory, you are responsible for knowing and obeying all of these. It is said that "ignorance is no excuse" for violating the law. But with so many laws, and the difficulty in even finding them, it's virtually impossible for anyone to be a model citizen. So, it should come as no surprise that over 70% of American adults have committed a crime that could land them in jail.[13]

Even as to the crimes most of us do know about, a large percentage of Americans have engaged in many of these. One example is the use or possession of marijuana (it's still a federal crime despite being "legalized" in many states). Another is downloading songs or movies without the permission of the rights holder. Of course, not all crimes are widely enforced, especially when so many people engage in them. Compare the over two-thirds of estimated Americans who have committed a crime to the percent of Americans who have a criminal record, which is about one-third.[14] There's simply not enough resources to do this enforcement – not enough police, or courts, or jails.

While you may think that as long as we are not putting half of the American population in jail for doing a little weed, the very fact that laws are on the books that people routinely violate is not a problem. Actually, it's a big problem.

As people with varying political views have argued, too many laws that too many people violate, weakens the rule of law.[15] This happens for two reasons. First, the respect people have for the law *in general* begins to erode over time. If a significant number of Americans decide it's perfectly acceptable to openly violate one law, what about other laws? Or if people become overwhelmed with trying to figure out what the law is, they may simply throw up their hands and forget it altogether. ¯_(ツ)_/¯

Second, when too many people are violating the law, law enforcement cannot prosecute everyone. They must decide who to go after. The natural tendency is to selectively enforce such crimes based on who they think "deserves" it more. This gives police and the government too much discretion. Officials may use this leeway to crack down harder on certain types of people based on race, politics, or other characteristics. It doesn't lend itself to the neutral and equal application of the law that we expect in a constitutional democracy.

Then there's the problem of too many rules that people *do* follow. When laws are too specific and too rigid, they can lead to some ridiculous results, as Barry Schwartz, a top psychologist and author argues.[16] In one dramatic example he cites, a father took his 11-year-old son to a baseball game. His son asked for some lemonade, so the father went to go buy some. They only had Mike's Hard Lemonade, which is 5% alcohol, but he didn't realize this, and gave it to his son. A security guard spotted the kid drinking it, and called the police, who called an ambulance to rush the boy to the emergency room.

> *"If you have ten thousand regulations, you destroy all respect for the law."*
>
> *— Winston Churchill*

The hospital found no alcohol in his blood, and was going to discharge him. Instead, the child welfare protection agency sent him to a foster home for three days. The agency finally allowed the boy to go home, but only if the dad left the house and checked into a hotel! Two weeks later, the situation was resolved.

How did things get so out of hand over an 11-year-old accidentally having a few sips of a 5% alcoholic drink? The welfare workers and the paramedics and the judge all apparently realized the overreaction; they all said something like: "we hate to do it, but we have to follow procedure." Too many strict laws and regulations required these professionals to take certain specified actions. The rules did not allow them to use their judgment.

Now that we understand the scope of the problem, let's discuss how it got to this point, and whether we may be able to fix it.

How it Got So Bad

The reality is that laws have proliferated for some good reasons, as we'll see. But there are some old laws that do not have any clear purpose or relevance to today's world. Indeed, many laws simply "fly under the radar." These may go years without being put to use or being considered for repeal.

Here's a fun example. Did you know in the city of Los Angeles, it's illegal to play the hurdy-gurdy on the street or sidewalk?[17] What's a hurdy-gurdy, you ask? According to Wikipedia, it's "a stringed instrument that produces sound by a hand crank-turned, rosined wheel rubbing against the strings."[18] Maybe there was some sort of good reason for banning this particular instrument at some point. Today, not so much.

But most laws in effect today have been created for arguably justifiable purposes. As discussed previously, complex systems spring up as a result of the complexity of human life and society. And the more complex society becomes, with an ever-increasing population, and more advanced technologies changing how people live, the more rules we may need.

One new technology is really complicating things on the streets. In the last few years, thousands of electric scooters have suddenly appeared in cities across the country. While they have increased options for mobility for many people, they also create new potential problems. Some scooter riders maneuver erratically through cars and pedestrians. Or they may haphazardly leave the scooters on sidewalks, making it more likely that people will trip over them and get hurt.

There are already laws about **negligence** where a person can sue for another person's lack of care which results in harm to the other person. But it's unclear how this would apply. Would the harmed person sue the one who left the scooter there (if they can be found)? Or sue the scooter company? Or both? What if the harmed person doesn't have the wherewithal to bring a lawsuit?

Might it be better to deal with the situation by trying to *prevent* the harm in the first place? Perhaps by penalizing the companies if they don't keep the sidewalks clear of scooters. Or even more drastically, banning the scooters altogether in certain areas, which some cities have done.

Then there's the wonderful mess that the internet has created, which lawmakers have struggled to tackle. One internet-enabled phenomenon is short-term rentals, like Airbnb. Some people love using these arrangements for travel or to make some extra money. But many residents storm their local government meetings, complaining about things like loud parties and trash, demanding bans or limits on Airbnb be put in place. It's a classic conflict between homeowners' rights to do what they want with their property, and quality of life issues which affect the neighbors.

These Airbnb bans are also vigorously supported by the hotel industry, as they see this new business model as disruptive to their profits. As one of the least justified purposes, laws are sometimes used for the wealthy and powerful to maintain their wealth and power.

Laws and regulations have also proliferated in an attempt to deal with the negative impacts of technology on our air, water, food, and overall environment. In the 1960s and 1970s, American cities were starting to look like Beijing does today

– thick with smog. Congress responded by passing the Clean Air Act, which implemented new emissions limits for cars, factories, and other sources of pollution. As a result, lead air pollution has decreased by 92% since 1980. And hundreds of millions of cases of respiratory and cardiovascular disease have been prevented.[19]

As climate change becomes more of a problem in our present and future, some state and local governments are passing laws and regulations in response (since Republicans in Congress refuse to do much on this). As an example, a California law requires all new housing to have solar panels installed. And the city of Berkeley has banned the use of natural gas in new homes. Some may see these measures as drastic, but given the likely dire consequences of climate change, doing nothing may be even more drastic.

The abundance of laws is not just the result of dealing with the problems created by technology. It's also related to cultural changes in attitudes. In general, we have become a more "protective" society, placing greater emphasis on preventing people from harming themselves and others. In the last several decades, laws have been passed requiring drivers and passengers to wear seatbelts, restricting the ability to obtain medication without a prescription, and even taxing or banning certain unhealthy foods like sugary sodas and trans fats.

Many people, particularly libertarians, deride these types of **paternalist** (or **maternalist**, if you will) laws as part of a **nanny state** that doesn't want people to face the consequences of their actions. However, since 1950, the death rate from accidental injuries has been cut in half. And the death rate from cardiovascular disease has been reduced to less than 1/3 of what it was![20] It's hard to say whether most of these deaths were prevented directly as a result of such laws, or whether it was mostly due to other factors. Yet it's likely that the laws helped somewhat.

Remember the fiasco of the child drinking the hard lemonade? There used to be general laws that said something to the effect of "use your best judgment for the welfare of the child." But some officials are lax in performing their jobs, leading to children being harmed or even killed upon going back to abusive households. Now, to try to prevent this harm, there are more specific new laws that say "if A happens, do XYZ," "if B happens, do ZYX," and so on.

More rules may help prevent disaster, but they may also lead to ridiculous and unfair results, like the father being separated from his child for two weeks. Is the solution to simply get rid of these rules? We have all these new rules because we no longer trust the judgment of certain professionals. But *should* we trust them? When we leave it up to judgment, there will always be some percentage of professionals who get it wrong. This will inevitably lead to more harm and deaths.

Those who want to get rid of all nanny state laws should be prepared to accept that this would almost certainly result in more injuries, disease, death, and other harms. Maybe it's worth it, in order to increase the level of freedom we have. Maybe not. We should at least have an honest conversation about this trade-off.

For all these reasons, that's how we get so many new laws all the time, all building up into a larger and larger collection. Even though most people would probably agree that the proliferation of laws is a problem, it is a hard problem to solve.

A Modest Proposal: Culture as Cure

In order to reduce the volume of laws, there is some low-hanging fruit to pick, which is old laws that are irrelevant in our modern society, but still on the books. On the other hand, once a law is on the books, it's difficult to get rid of it. There's simply not as much energy for removing unnecessary laws as there is for creating new ones. Perhaps we need some regular "cleanup" mechanism in which a commission meets every few years to suggest laws to sweep up.

Another way to address the issue is to change the focus from laws to culture. We may be relying too much on laws and government to do some of the work that culture should be doing. The system of rules and enforcement cannot possibly solve all problems. And it could be counterproductive, as people and companies tend to resist constraints being imposed on them. People will always try to find their way around the rules. Remember that humans rejected the tyranny of the chimpanzee world.

Instead of this top-down approach, people may be more responsive to a bottom-up approach in which they collaborate to prevent or alleviate problems they may be responsible for. Many of these rules could be replaced by a stronger culture of ethics and norms based on human-centered values. This could help create a society that works better for everyone, and also reduce the number of laws and the complexity of government.

While many may say it is naïve to believe that a corporation which is polluting the environment will somehow "see the light" and regulate itself, this is not what I'm arguing. Rather, corporations respond primarily to one thing – profits – and that's where we come in. We, the consumers, are starting to demand more from companies that we patronize or don't patronize. It looks like it's working. The social enterprise and B Corporation movement is growing rapidly.[21] And a lobbying group of the country's leading CEOs recently declared for the first time that the interests of the community and employees are just as important as those of the shareholders.[22]

It remains to be seen whether this culture shift will indeed have a lasting major impact or not. I'm cautiously optimistic.

Section 5: How Did We Get Here: A Recap

It has been a long road to get to where we are now, and yet we have a long way to go. In the U.S., our justice system, while not yet entirely fair, is at least an improvement on systems that existed in history and that still exist in many countries. We have a democratic government which affords the opportunity, at least in theory, to make things more fair for everyone.

The system is far from perfect, and we still have more work to do. But it's important to reflect how far humans have come from the days of the Hammurabi Code and the monarchies of the Middle Ages, and even the early semi-democracies of the ancient Greeks and Romans.

Humans began using government and laws primarily for maintaining order. The systems soon came to be used for many other purposes, both positive, nefarious, and something in between. These range from protecting basic human rights and promoting fairness, imposing forced slave labor, carrying out genocide, preventing people from harming themselves, and dealing with problems caused by technology.

Laws have accumulated over time in order to accomplish many of these goals. And even though most of the law exists for arguably justifiable purposes, the sheer volume and complexity of the law threatens the fabric of the system. Leveraging our cultural and consumer power may serve as a preferable alternative to some regulations.

Maintaining a stable society that works for everyone is not easy. Although in historical terms we have done quite well so far, we must recognize that even our own system is fragile. We have seen democracies come and go throughout history. It is up to all of us to ensure that law and government are used to benefit the people, and that the system does not become too weak or too strong.

Despite our progress towards a more fair and just society, many people across the world still live in systems with brutal conditions. To paraphrase the Declaration of Independence, all people are created equal (well actually it said "all *men* are created equal" but let's go ahead and update that). But this sentiment is not just an American ideal, and the goal of developing and maintaining well-functioning legal and governmental systems is not just an American project, but a human project.

Article 2:
How Does the Legal and Government System Work (or Not Work)?

Article 2: How Does the Legal and Government System Work (or Not Work)?

Any properly functioning legal and government system must do three main things with law: (1) create and repeal laws; (2) interpret and apply (or don't apply) laws to specific situations; and (3) implement and enforce (or choose not to enforce) laws in certain situations. These three functions generally map on to the three branches of government: legislative, judicial, and executive, respectively. While these functions are *primarily* carried out by the respective branch, in reality all branches do all functions on some level. Before we take a closer look at the system, a quick note about how the federal and the state governments fit together.

What are the Levels of Government?

There are three basic levels of government: national (aka federal), state, and local. The federal government acts on behalf of the country as a whole. Each state also has its own government system, which operates independently of the federal government. The earliest states, after independence from Britain, began as essentially their own countries. Even later on, Texas, California, and Hawaii were their own countries for varying periods of time. As states were incorporated into the country, they maintained significant control over many areas of law and governance. But they are still subject to federal laws, including the U.S. Constitution. This overlay of the federal and state systems is called **federalism**.

The local levels, including counties and cities, are considered subdivisions of the state. Although they may have substantial autonomy from the state government, the local level is not considered an independent level of government.

While media coverage focuses on issues of national importance, don't be fooled. Most laws and government actions that affect people on a day-to-day basis originate at the state and local levels. The infographic on the next page shows the structure of federalism and the three branches in each level of government.

Section 1: Who's in Charge Here?

Law is King

What does it mean that nobody is above the law?

Government officials cannot simply do whatever they want. All government action is constrained by the U.S. Constitution, state constitutions, and other laws. By this point you know why, right? Rule of law. We are governed by laws, not by officials.

WHAT DO OUR LEADERS EVEN DO?

	LEGISLATIVE BRANCH (MAKES LAWS)	EXECUTIVE BRANCH (IMPLEMENTS & ENFORCES LAWS)	JUDICIAL BRANCH (INTERPRETS & APPLIES LAWS)
FEDERAL	CONGRESS (SENATE & HOUSE OF REPRESENATTIVES)	PRESIDENT VICE PRESIDENT ATTORNEY GENERAL FBI MILITARY OTHER FEDERAL AGENCIES	U.S. SUPREME COURT COURTS OF APPEAL DISTRICT COURTS
STATE	STATE LEGISLATURE (STATE SENATE & STATE HOUSE)	GOVERNOR STATE ATTORNEY GENERAL OTHER STATE AGENCIES NATIONAL GUARD STATE POLICE	STATE SUPREME COURT STATE APPEALS COURT STATE TRIAL COURT
LOCAL	COUNTY GOVERNMENT CITY COUNCIL	MAYOR COUNTY GOVERNMENT SHERIFF/ LOCAL POLICE LOCAL AGENCIES DISTRICT ATTORNEY	LOCAL COURTS (SOME STATES)

The U.S. Constitution is the primary way that the power of government and government officials is limited. While individuals, companies, and other entities outside of the government are subject to the law in general, they are *not* directly subject to the U.S. Constitution. Because the government has such a strong ability to impact the lives of citizens, this document focuses its attention on those in these positions of power.

When government steps over the line, whether that line is drawn by the Constitution or other laws, it's primarily the job of the courts to declare when that line has been crossed, and the job of the executive to enforce this. The courts have the power to declare government actions as **unconstitutional**, and to block those actions. And when officials violate criminal laws, the courts can sentence them to jail, just as with private citizens.

Are government officials shielded from prosecution for crimes?

Generally, no. However, a Department of Justice memo asserts that the president cannot be prosecuted while still in office. He or she must first be impeached and removed from office, and *then* prosecuted. The reasoning is that a trial would interfere with the president's important duties and could be a threat to national security. But the courts have never taken up this issue.

"In America, the law is king. For as in absolute governments the King is law, so in free countries the law ought to be king"

– *Thomas Paine, Common Sense, 1776*

What is a Law, Anyway?

A law is any rule or order that requires someone to do or not do something, and which can be enforced by a court and law enforcement. Most people think of laws as simply those passed by Congress or state legislatures, which are called **statutes**. But there are many types of laws, including those created by courts and executives, as we will see.

Sometimes a "law" is not a law at all! When a court invalidates a law because it is unconstitutional or is otherwise invalid, it no longer has the **force of law**, meaning, it can no longer be enforced. The law has lost its essence, its life force, its joie de vivre, if you will. Other examples of legal documents that do not have the force of law are **guidance documents** published by the government, **memos** written by the Department of Justice, or contracts that a court deems invalid.

While "law is king," laws are created by humans, of course (can we please agree never to delegate this to an AI algorithm?). Laws are created either by a body or person with some official authority to do so. In a sense, these institutions are the king-makers, or the king's right-hand (and left-hand), if you will. The next section discusses the various types of laws or actions with the force of law, and how they are created.

Section 2: Who Makes the Rules Around Here?

The classic *Schoolhouse Rock!* video "I'm Just a Bill" about how a bill becomes a law is an excellent explanation of how Congress and the President enact laws. But this is not the only way to make a law. Here are the various ways laws are created, and the people or entities that create them:

1. Legislative Bodies – Makin' the Law

Lawmakers are also called **legislators**, and together, legislators form a body called a **legislature**. Congress, the state legislatures, city councils, and other local legislative government create **legislation**, aka **statutes**, aka **public laws**. With the power to make laws also comes the power to unmake, or **repeal** them. These are the superpowers of government. And yet, Congress is not exactly filled with superheroes.

Legislatures don't usually act alone. The respective executive (e.g. the president or governor) has the power to **veto**, or reject bills they don't like. However, Congress and most other legislatures can override the veto with a certain percentage of votes (two thirds (2/3) of both houses, in the case of Congress).

When Congress passes legislation, it is called a **federal statute**. These are compiled into the **U.S. Code**, which is the book of all the federal statutes currently in force. When a state legislature passes legislation, it is called a **state statute**. These are compiled into state law codes. When a local government, including county legislature or city council, passes legislation, it is usually called an **ordinance** or **local law**. These are compiled into what may be called a **county code** or **municipal code**, or **administrative code**.

How do legislatures work?

Within a legislature, there are often two separate bodies, called houses, that must work together to make laws. Congress contains two houses (**bicameral**, if we're being fancy) – the Senate and the House of Representatives. And every state except Nebraska has two houses. At the local level, almost every city council or county government has just one house (**unicameral**).

The reason to have two separate parts of a legislature is to have another layer of checks and balances, and to slow things down a bit (the U.S. Senate is highly proficient at keeping things not moving). In two-house legislatures, there is generally an upper house, always called a Senate, and lower house, often called the House of Representatives, House of Delegates, or Assembly.

Sometimes referred to as the "cooling chamber" (sounds like a spa treatment), the upper house is expected to chill the passions of the "rowdy" people in the lower house. Senators, whether in the U.S. Senate or state senates, serve longer terms of office (four to six years), and represent more citizens, compared to the lower house. Because they don't need to worry about reelection as often, and usually have a broader base of voters, Senators tend to be more politically centrist and willing to compromise.

The U.S. Senate and some state senates have yet another tool to slow things down, which has received plenty of attention in recent years: the **filibuster**. As with so many word origin stories, the one for "filibuster" paints a perfect picture of what the word means today. From the French *flibustier* and the Spanish *filibustero*, it originally described adventurers who incited revolutions in Latin America in order to disrupt the functions of these governments.[23] Now it signifies an attempt by a group of Senators to disrupt the functioning of the U.S. Senate, specifically by blocking certain legislation from even being voted on.

It works as follows. Generally, if a simple majority of the Senators vote for a piece of legislation, it passes that house. This number is usually 51, unless there is a 50-50 tie, in which case the Vice President breaks the tie. Before a vote takes place on the legislation, there is time for debate on the issue. There must be at least 60 Senators to vote to end debate and move on to the voting part. So, if at least 40 Senators really-super-for-sure don't want the legislation to pass, they can simply refuse to vote to stop debate, and there will never be a vote on that issue. A clever trick, eh?

The filibuster has often been used to prevent a vote on many pieces of legislation which otherwise would have passed, as they had the support of a majority of Senators. Many political observers now expect that it takes at least 60 votes in the Senate to get almost anything passed.

As for lower houses, they have their own issues. Members of lower houses are considered more subject to the whims and passions of the population. This is because they generally have short two-years terms in office, and thus are always trying to give the people what they want in order to be re-elected soon. They also represent fewer citizens, who may be more homogenous and ideologically extreme.

Can legislatures make laws about whatever they want?

No. The Constitution specifies various powers of Congress, and leaves the rest to the states. A few powers Congress has are the power to declare war (you thought this was the president's decision, right?), the power to set and collect taxes, and regulate commerce.

In contrast, states legislatures can pass laws on almost anything, except when it interferes with federal laws or programs, or anything expressly prohibited by the U.S. Constitution or state constitution.

Local legislatures are given certain legislative powers by the state, and vary widely in what they can do. They certainly

How Does the Legal and Government System Work? 49

cannot make laws in conflict with state or federal laws, or the Constitution. They vary even as to what they are called. At the county level, there may be a Board of Supervisors, or County Commission, County Council, or something similar. At the city level, the legislature is usually the city council.

2. Executive as Lawmaker Lite

As discussed above, executives, including the president, governors, and mayors, generally play a role in creating **legislation**, by either signing or vetoing it. But most lawmaking bodies also have the power to **override the veto**, if they get a certain percentage of support (usually 2/3). In addition to veto power, the executive regularly (usually each year) asks the legislature for money for the executive agencies. The legislature can approve, deny, or modify this budget, sending it back to the executive to sign (or veto).

Executives can also issue **executive actions** or **executive orders** to their **administration**, which consists of all the departments which carry out government functions.

Executive agencies

Government agencies or departments, such as the Environmental Protection Agency (EPA), are created and given missions by statutes. The statutes are usually not very specific about how the agency should carry out its mission. To fill in these gaps, the agency is authorized to issue **rules and regulations**, which companies and individuals must follow. The federal rules and regulations are all found in the **U.S. Code of Federal Regulations (CFR)**.

3. Courts Play Lawmaker, Too

When courts issue **judgments** or decisions in a case, these form the body of **case law.** These decisions often involve interpreting other types of law, including statutes, and rules and regulations, and applying them to the case. If there are no relevant statutes or rules and regulations, courts must decide the case by creating their own law, which is known as **common law**.

4. Founders of Country or State – the OGs

The Founding Fathers of the United States drafted the **U.S. Constitution**, and the founders of each of the 50 states created their **state constitutions**, which set out **constitutional laws** for how the government can and cannot operate. Of course, we are not simply bound forever to the words written by a few people several hundred years ago. The U.S. Constitution can be amended through action by Congress and the state legislatures together. This has been done 27 times so far. And each state constitution has its own process for amending these state documents.

5. Voters – Yes, That's You

Here's where you get to play lawmaker. Many (but not all) states and local governments allow for voters to create laws *directly* by voting on **ballot measures** or **propositions**. These are also known as **referendums**, and if approved, ultimately become a **statute** or **ordinance**. There are no national referendums, although many other countries do have this practice.

6. Parties to a Contract: A Private Show

By mutual agreement to a contract, individuals and/or companies can create their own **private laws** between themselves and other parties to the contract. They are known as private laws in contrast to the public laws which apply to the general public.

"Law never is, but is always about to be."

- Benjamin Cardozo, Supreme Court Justice

Section 3: Who Enforces the Rules Around Here?

Just as there are many ways laws can be created, there are many ways laws are enforced. There are the officials who actually lock people up; and when courts decide who wins or loses a case, this is a form of enforcing the law.

1. Executive: Enforcer-in-Chief

As the primary enforcer of the laws (both civil and criminal), the executive plays a major role in the legal system. The executive branch includes federal, state, and local executives and law enforcement.

It is generally impossible to enforce all laws against all violators at all times. Thus, executives generally have the power of **prosecutorial discretion**. This simply means that they can prioritize enforcement of certain laws over others, or more serious violators over others.

Related to prosecutorial discretion is the **commutation power** and **pardon power**. When an executive pardons someone who has committed a crime, the pardoned individual is not required to serve any jail time or other punishment, and is essentially cleared of wrongdoing. It's truly a Get Out of Jail Free card. An executive can also commute someone's sentence, which means they get out of jail early, but they still have a criminal record.

The president can pardon or commute anyone for federal crimes, but not for crimes based on state or local laws. Most governors have the power to pardon or commute people for state or local crimes.

How does the executive branch work?

Enforcement of criminal laws occurs primarily through three main functions: 1) investigation and arrest; 2) prosecuting the suspect in court, making the case that the suspect is guilty of the crime charged; and 3) punishment, including running the jails. Enforcement of civil (non-criminal) laws is generally done through executive agencies, involving fines and other penalties.

There are various players within the executive, so it can get a little tricky. But you need to know who to call if local police aren't doing their job to protect you, and you need to know why the FBI might be showing up at your door.

What is a "state of emergency" declaration?

Executives at the national, state, and even local levels can declare a **state of emergency** for various reasons. It is often used to immediately divert funds into an area of priority, such as relief after a natural or human-made disaster.

Under the National Emergencies Act, the president can activate various special powers, ranging from suspending laws regulating chemical and biological weapons, including the ban on human testing; to suspending the Clean Air Act; to authorizing and constructing military construction projects using any existing defense appropriations for such military constructions. However, wary of this extraordinary amount of power, courts have rejected some emergency declarations as overstepping the executive's authority.

Who are our federal officials?

At the federal level, executive power is primarily concentrated in the president, as he or she is the only elected executive official, who then appoints the rest of the officials. However, even though the president appoints the United States attorney general, the attorney general is expected to maintain some independence from the president, in order to avoid conflicts of interest. This is because the attorney general is responsible for investigating the rest of the executive branch, including the president (usually through an independently appointed **special counsel** when necessary).

The president is **commander-in-chief** of the military, and it is very important that the civilian government maintains control over this institution with enormous capabilities of physical force. Still, the military's oath is to uphold the Constitution, not loyalty to the president. Officers have the responsibility to refuse unlawful orders.

While the purpose of the military is primarily to defend the country from foreign threats, in emergency situations, the president can use the military or the National Guard to keep the peace within the country. In a dramatic showdown in 1963, President John Kennedy ordered the Alabama

National Guard to protect two black students who were trying to enroll at the University of Alabama. The Alabama governor at the time was physically blocking the door to the school, in defiance of the Supreme Court decision in *Brown vs. Board of Education* which declared segregation in education illegal. Only because of the military presence did the governor back down. It is clear that the president has quite extraordinary power to enforce the laws, even against other governmental entities.

The U.S. attorney general is in charge of the Department of Justice, which carries out most of the regular law enforcement activities at the federal level. Within the Department of Justice are various enforcement agencies, including the Federal Bureau of Investigation (FBI), the Drug Enforcement Administration (DEA), and the Bureau of Alcohol, Tobacco, Firearms and Explosives (ATF). While the DEA and ATF have more specific missions, the FBI is basically the federal police department which investigates and arrests people for general federal crimes. After an arrest is made, a U.S. attorney at the Department of Justice will determine whether to prosecute the case in federal court.

Executive agencies

Executive agencies enforce their own **originating statutes** and **rules and regulations**. Executive agencies that enforce civil laws do so mostly through issuing fines to violators. For example, the Environmental Protection Agency (EPA) may impose a fine on a business that is polluting more than is legally allowed.

Who are my state officials?

As powerful as the federal executive is, it's important to note, once again, that most laws are created and enforced at the state and local level. At the state and local levels, executive power is more widely distributed than at the federal level. While the only federal executive elected to office is the president, states and local governments generally elect other executive offices separately.

The top level is the governor, always elected. The governor has control of the state's police force, and shares control (with the president) of the state's National Guard.

Each state also has its own attorney general, in charge of the state's Department of Justice. But in contrast to the federal system, almost every state elects its attorney general separately. Attorneys at the Department of Justice may prosecute violations of state criminal and civil law in state court. There are often other statewide executives that are elected separately, such as the head of elections (often called the state's Secretary of State) and other affairs.

State and local elections officials are responsible for the fair and impartial administration of elections. Unfortunately, in recent years, some of these officials, particularly on the

Right, have embraced false claims of widespread voter fraud, using it to justify their willingness to overturn the will of the voters. This may be the gravest threat to our system right now. We must keep a close watch on these officials and vote them out or otherwise keep them out of office.

Who are my local officials?

The structure of the executive at the local level varies a bit from state to state and even by region within a state. Counties and cities are political **subdivisions** of the state. The state grants counties and cities the power to pass their own laws on local issues, and to maintain their own administrations. In most states, cities sit within the boundaries of a county, but the city may operate mostly independently of the county. Sometimes, like in New York City, it's the reverse, where five counties sit inside the megacity. And at least one county and city are one and the same – the city and county of San Francisco.

Large cities usually elect their mayor, and other executive positions like the **city attorney**, who investigates both civil and criminal violations within the city. A city may have its own police force, usually under the mayor's control. As an example, the Los Angeles City mayor appoints the **chief of police** of the LAPD; the NYPD calls its head the **chief of department**.

Smaller cities and towns are usually under the jurisdiction of the **county sheriff**, who is generally elected independently. The **district attorney** ("DA"), the local prosecutor, is usually elected at the county level. After the sheriff or local police arrest a suspect, the district attorney determines whether to prosecute the suspect in state court.

City or county agencies also enforce civil violations, often through fines. If you drive a car, you are almost certainly familiar with this experience – when a parking ticket shows up on your windshield!

2. Legislatures as Enforcer

Legislatures also have some enforcement powers. Congress can hold hearings and investigate people and organizations for potential violations of law, and can hold people in **contempt of Congress** for refusing to cooperate with an investigation. Congress can also **impeach** and remove federal officials, including the president and judges, giving Congress a vast power to check and balance against the other branches.

3. Courts as Enforcer

Applying the law and deciding that a person has violated it, and what the punishment should be, is also a form of enforcement.

What happens if someone disobeys a court order?

If a judge issues a judgment in a case, and the person ordered to do something (or not do something) disobeys this, the judge can find the person in **contempt of court**. The judge can then have the person arrested and sent to jail. This applies to everyone, including government officials.

"The Court stands against any winds that blow as havens of refuge for those who might otherwise suffer because they are helpless, weak, outnumbered, or because they are nonconforming victims of prejudice or public excitement."

*- Hugo Black,
Supreme Court Justice*

Section 4: Who Says What the Law is?

As we have seen, various players *write* and *implement* the laws. But words on a page don't mean much without a way to ensure that people are following them. And no matter how many words are written describing the rules, the complexities of life mean that there are always situations where it is unclear if a law applies or not.

The institutions in charge of deciding how the laws apply to the real world are primarily the courts, and secondarily, the executive.

1. Courts as Interpreters of Law

The courts, particularly the U.S. Supreme Court, have the ultimate say on what the law means. For example, if a federal agency imposes a penalty against Corp, Inc. for violating a regulation, Corp, Inc. can appeal to the U.S. District Court, which can issue a **judgment** that Corp, Inc. did *not* violate that regulation. This would then overrule the penalty.

How do the courts work?

The judicial branch, also referred to as simply the Judiciary, consists of the federal court system, and the state court system, which operate independently. Importantly, federal courts decide whether laws and other governmental actions violate the Constitution – whether they are **unconstitutional** – or not. Federal and state courts also decide whether government officials have properly followed federal, state, or local law or not. The courts also use the law to resolve disputes between private citizens, declaring winners and losers.

These powers essentially give the courts a veto over the rest of the government, and significant influence on our lives. Of course, these decisions are not simply based on the judges' own preference. At least, they aren't generally supposed to be. The job of a judge is to simply "call balls and strikes." And a major rule of the game says that courts must make their decisions based on decisions other courts made in prior similar cases, known as **precedent**.

That said, sometimes courts explicitly declare that precedent was wrongly decided, and that it must be overturned. For example, in the 1944 case of Korematsu vs. U.S., the Supreme Court ruled that the internment of Japanese Americans during World War II was constitutional. It was not until 2018 that the Supreme Court repudiated this precedential decision as wrong.[24]

Sometimes there are cases which are entirely novel and there is no relevant precedent. In this situation, it is truly within the court's purview to decide what the law *should be*. This judge-made law is called **common law**. Judges look to historical and foreign examples, as well as a general sense of fairness, to decide what the law should be.

> *"The judge, even when he is free, is still not wholly free. He is not to innovate at pleasure. He is not a knight-errant, roaming at will in pursuit of his own ideal of beauty or of goodness."*
>
> - *Benjamin Cardozo, Supreme Court Justice*

Aren't judges just politicians in robes?

Unlike the legislative and executive branches, the judiciary is not considered a political branch. Judges must make decisions as objectively as possible. They should not be subject to the influences of politics. The independence of judges is one of the most important principles of the system. They must be free to strike down laws and actions by elected officials when their best legal judgment demands it.

The importance of judicial independence is why federal judges are not *elected*, but instead are *appointed* by the president, with approval by the Senate. Federal judges are appointed for life, and cannot be removed except for impeachment for serious crimes, or voluntary retirement.

While judges are supposed to be non-political, many legal observers believe that judges in practice often make decisions in line with their politics and the politics of the person who appointed them. Still, some judges are less ideological than others, and make decisions that contradict what you would expect based on who appointed them.

Legal scholars also believe that the courts, particularly the Supreme Court, at least consider public sentiment in their decision making. Courts see it as vital to maintaining legitimacy in the eyes of the public.

There are nine judges (technically called **justices**) on the U.S. Supreme Court. Although many people believe that this number of justices is "set in stone," or at least in the Constitution, this is not the case. Congress can change this number at any time. In fact, they did so multiple times between 1801 and 1869, at one point reaching 10 justices. For some reason, after 1869, Congress stopped tinkering with the number of seats on the Supreme Court. This gave us the situation today in which every time one of them dies or retires, the process of the new appointment becomes a dramatic political spectacle.

One of the president's most significant powers is being able to appoint judges and thus shape the courts in her or his image, which can last several decades into the future. Those in opposition to the president are left hoping that their favored judges will hold on for dear life until the president is out of office (RIP RBG).

These high stakes could be substantially reduced if certain reforms were imposed. One way to fix it would be to simply increase the number of seats on the court. But this is a highly controversial idea at this point. In the 1930s, President Franklin Roosevelt tried to get Congress to add up to six additional justices. His plan was criticized as an attempt to "pack the court" in order to give himself more power over the Court.

To mitigate this concern, perhaps the new justices could be appointed by an independent commission, instead of the president. This would require a constitutional amendment, but this reform would go a long way towards improving the health of the entire legal and government system.

State courts operate quite differently from the federal system. Only a few states appoint judges for life. Most state judges are *elected* to their judgeships, or at least must face a **retention election** a certain number of years after being appointed to their office.[25] A retention election involves a simple yes or no vote, rather than competing against other candidates.

Many legal scholars have criticized this mixing of judges and politics that occurs in many states as a threat to fair and impartial justice.[26] Studies have found strong correlations between the donors to a judge's campaign and the judge's rulings.[27] Although the state courts, like the federal courts, are not considered part of the political branches, one could argue that these elections do indeed insert state courts into the political system.

This is a problem with a relatively simple solution – judges should only be appointed, not elected. Unfortunately, many voters either don't understand the importance of judicial independence, or don't care. They prefer to assert their ideological leanings on the courts.

How do federal courts work?

Federal courts only take cases related to federal laws, including the U.S. Constitution. If a case includes both a federal issue and a state issue, a federal court may decide both issues. Federal cases start out at one of the 94 District Courts spread throughout the country, with between one and three District Courts per state.

The "loser" of a case in District Court may appeal to the U.S. Court of Appeals, of which there are 13 **circuits** around the country, each with jurisdiction over 5-10 states. For example, the 9th Circuit Court of Appeals sits in San Francisco, and hears appeals from California, Arizona, Nevada, Oregon, Washington, Idaho, and Montana.

> *"The success of any legal system is measured by its fidelity to the universal ideal of justice."*
>
> *- Earl Warren, Supreme Court Justice*

Usually, the Court of Appeals is the end of the road for most cases. While the loser at the Circuit Court of Appeals may appeal to the U.S. Supreme Court, this highest court is not obligated to take the case. The Supreme Court could not possibly handle the caseload of the roughly 10,000 cases per year it is requested to hear. In fact, the U.S. Supreme Court takes less than 2% of the cases requested.

The Supreme Court generally takes cases it considers the most nationally significant, or in order to resolve conflicting opinions between the Circuit Courts of Appeals. To take a case, which is called granting it a **writ of certiorari**, at least four of the nine justices must agree to hear it.

How do state courts work?

As mentioned previously, most laws are created at the state and local level, which laws are generally interpreted by state courts, not federal courts. The vast majority of cases (95%) go through the state court system.[28] Although the state court systems vary, generally they have three levels: the trial court, appeals court, and state high court.

The state trial court is usually called the Superior Court, District Court, or Circuit Court (but in New York, the trial court is confusingly called the Supreme Court!). The appeals court is usually just called the Appeals Court (or Appellate Division).

Just about every state calls its highest court the Supreme Court, except that the high court in Maryland, New York, and Washington, DC is called the Court of Appeals. Like the federal courts, most of the state supreme courts also take most of their cases at their discretion. Thus, quite often the state appeals court is the last bite at the apple.

However, sometimes even the state high court is not the last stop. If there is a federal issue involved, the loser may appeal to the U.S. Supreme Court, which, as discussed above, may or may not decide to take up the case. If the U.S. Supreme Court does take the case, it can overrule the state high court on the federal issues.

2. Executive as Interpreter of Law

In order to carry out and enforce the laws, the executive must first decide what the law means. Police officers exercise this judgment every day when they determine whether crimes are being or have been committed. If an officer sees a person punch another, is the first person guilty of assault and battery? What if he was acting in self-defense? The executive must decide these questions, and act accordingly. Later, the courts may decide the executive is wrong, and may strike down the executive's actions.

Executive Agencies

Agencies at all levels of government generally have the power to determine what their own **originating statutes** and regulations mean. In this way, the agency can act like a court in that its **administrative law judges** can issue **administrative rulings** to decide whether a particular individual or company has violated the agency's statutes or rules and regulations. But the judiciary can overturn the agency's decisions.

Section 5: Whose Law is it, Anyway?

Of the various players involved in the system of making, enforcing, and interpreting laws – Congress, the president, the Supreme Court, governors, state legislatures, state courts, the voters and The People, the founders (and the

Constitution they wrote) – who is at the top of the heap? Well, nobody really. That's kind of the point; it's all about **checks and balances** so that nobody has too much power.

Although all power theoretically flows from The People, even The People are checked and balanced, as we will see. That said, some players do have more power than others, at least in certain domains, and in some circumstances. When enough of The People get together and want to make a change, they become the strongest entity in the system.

Another form of checks and balances, **federalism** divides the powers of government between the federal government and the states. While the federal government generally supersedes the state governments on many issues, this is not always the case.

The Constitution grants to Congress only specific **enumerated powers** on specific issues, including: commerce and economic issues that affect multiple states; trade with foreign countries; immigration; bankruptcy; copyright; the military and declaring war. Under the 10th Amendment, all other powers are "reserved to the States respectively, or to the people." Federal officials do have higher authority than the states on these enumerated powers. On all other issues, such as most criminal law, family law, or education, the states are in charge. This reserving of powers to the states is often referred to as **states' rights**.

But even on these issues, the states must comply with the federal Constitution, so the U.S. Supreme Court always has this power over the states. Also, if any issue even remotely (even very remotely) may affect the national economy, Congress can regulate it, not the states. This is because the Supreme Court has interpreted the Congressional power to regulate interstate business (aka the **interstate commerce clause**) very broadly.

In 1942, the Court even upheld a federal regulation that prohibited farmers from growing too much wheat for their own home consumption![29] The rationale was that, if all farmers did this, a significant amount of wheat would not be sold on the market, thus affecting interstate wheat market.

Another major way Congress exercises its power over the states is its **funding power**. The federal government provides a significant amount of money to the states for various programs. It can attach strings to this money such that if the states do not take certain actions, the Feds can withhold the funds.

Take the minimum age for drinking alcohol, for example. There is no federal law directly establishing the minimum age as 21 years old. Instead, the federal government threatened to withdraw federal highway funding from the states if they didn't impose this minimum age. (Note: a lower drinking age is connected with fewer accidents and deaths on the roads).

Congress's expanded use of the commerce clause and funding power means that it can now make laws on almost any issue. Thus, Congress has very broad powers compared to the states.

As for the local level, cities and counties are always subordinate to the state level. But states often explicitly delegate certain authority or grant local control. Local government has a major impact on our day-to-day lives, and in some ways even more than the state or federal level.

A major local issue involves regulating the use of land, known as **zoning** and **land use**. This determines the layout of a city, affecting how easy or hard it is to get around. Zoning can also affect how much housing gets built, which can, in turn, affect the rent or price of a home. It's basic supply and demand. Is the rent "too damn high"? Rent control helps, but only for those currently in an apartment and who never want to move. To help lower the rent for everyone, local governments must allow new housing to be built.

The question of who is in charge is a wonderfully messy situation, and difficult to neatly represent on a diagram. For the sake of simplicity, the diagram on the next page shows The People at the top, who elect or otherwise have direct influence on the federal, state, and local governments. It also shows the federal government as having higher authority than the state government, which in turn has higher authority than the local government.

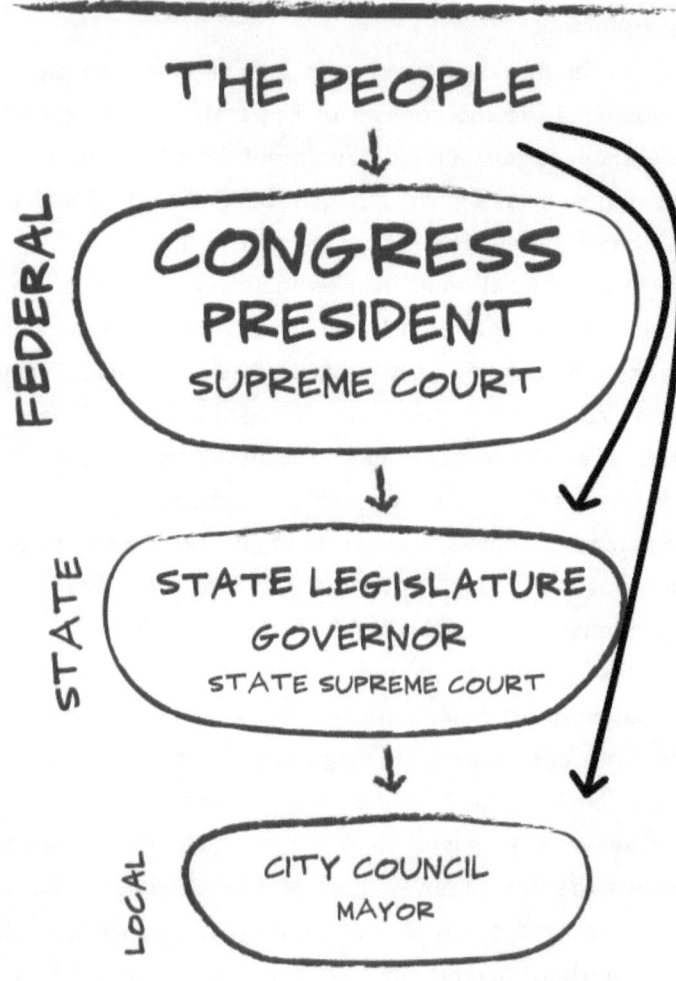

Who are The People?

The Preamble of the U.S. Constitution starts with three words: "We the People." This begs the question: who are **the People**, exactly? It's a romanticized notion that conjures up images of comradery and unity, as if we are all in unanimous agreement on how to govern ourselves. Of course, it's not so simple. First of all, it is virtually impossible to get 100% of the people to agree on anything. A democracy cannot function by unanimous consent.

When the Constitution was to be **ratified** by the state legislatures, it required a **simple majority**, that is, 50% plus one (or 51% to simplify) of each legislature to be approved. So then is it to be understood that We the People actually means "We *a simple majority of* the People"? OK, but what about the 49%? Are they then excluded from the People? Those who rejected the Constitution were nevertheless forced to submit to a brand new system of government that they didn't want.

Then there's the fact that the Constitution was never directly voted on by the general public. Only the state legislators had a say, who were generally elected only by white male property owners over the age of 21. Which was actually a small minority of the population. So, now we are to interpret the phrase as "We *a simple majority of state legislators who represent a small minority of* the People."

These days, while almost every adult citizen has the right to vote, often fewer than half actually do so, whether due to apathy or voter suppression tactics. Thus, in reality, a minority of the population is imposing decisions on the rest of the population.

> *"We in America do not have government by the majority. We have government by the majority who participate."*
>
> *— Thomas Jefferson*

Setting aside the issue of the voters not necessarily being representative of the population as a whole, my point is that whenever we talk about the People deciding this or that, we must remember that there are always some people who do not agree with that decision. The reality is that a pure **majoritarian** system means that some of the people will always be able to impose their will on the other people. This leads to a **tyranny of the majority** that tramples the rights of the minority.

Fortunately, we do not have a pure majoritarian system, as the Constitution grants the courts the power and duty to protect certain fundamental rights of the minority. (Ironically, a simple majority vote created a system in which simple majorities do not have ultimate authority). That minority can even be a single person; that person still deserves protection of the law. This is the concept of **individual rights**, and once again, our old friend, rule of law.

Rule of law often involves limiting the power of the people. Or more specifically, limiting the power of some of the people to infringe on the rights of the other people. Nobody is above the law, not even the People.

Further limits on democracy

The Founders did not trust the masses to make good decisions about governing. In the Constitutional framework for the federal government, the power of the people is never exercised directly, but is always moderated through various layers.

Indeed, we do not have a **direct democracy**, in which the population directly votes on every issue of public policy. We have a **representative democracy**, also known as a **republic**, in which voters vote for representatives, who in turn vote on issues of policy. When Benjamin Franklin was asked what type of government was created after the Constitutional Convention in 1787, he replied "a republic, if you can keep it." Over 200 years later we are still going, but we must continue to heed Franklin's words.

In many countries, voters can vote directly on constitutional amendments, laws, or other major questions. This process is generally called a **referendum** or **proposition**.[30] In the U.S., no direct democracy exists at the national level, although 26 states, and many cities and counties have some form of ballot measure or proposition system.[31]

But is direct democracy a good thing? Can the people be trusted to vote on specific issues on which they may not have adequate knowledge? Or does it just interfere with the "professional" work of lawmaking? Lawmakers, or at least their staffs, usually study proposed legislation carefully, including potential intended and unintended consequences. It is true that lawmakers screw it up sometimes as well, but at least they are better equipped to make public policy.

The Founders went so far – probably too far – as to prevent the direct election of U.S. Senators and the president. While U.S. Senators are now directly elected, the president is still not directly elected by the American people. Instead, the president is chosen through the convoluted system of the **Electoral College**. The Constitution provides that state legislatures can allocate their Electoral votes and choose the Electors (yes, the Electors are real people) however they want. Originally, the state legislatures would vote for the president, without consulting the population. Now, they generally allocate their Electoral votes to whoever wins the popular vote in the state.

While this method has evolved to reflect the will of a majority of voters of each state, it still does not reflect the will of the American people as a whole. Four presidents have been elected without winning the most votes nationwide. This reduces the legitimacy of the presidency, which reduces respect for the entire system.

Super powerful supermajorities

Another method for limiting the power of some of us to impose their will on the rest of us is to require a higher percentage of the people to approve a policy before it goes into effect. When the voting threshold is higher than a simple majority, often two-thirds or three-fourths, this is called a **supermajority** requirement.

Even direct democracy can be a proper method of decision making if the threshold is high enough. I suggest 75% is the right number, although in this polarized time, it seems near impossible to get to that level of agreement. Still, there are issues on which Americans overwhelmingly agree. On the question of universal background checks for gun purchases, 92% of voters support it![32] Despite this broad consensus, Congress has not enacted this policy into law. I won't go into why this is the case (*cough*: the NRA), but this issue is a perfect example of how direct democracy and the power of the people could be effectuated in a positive way.

A purported supermajority is required to amend the Constitution. Amendment procedures call for two alternative methods: (1) a two-thirds (2/3) vote of both houses of Congress, plus approval by three quarters (¾) of the states (generally through simple majority votes by state legislatures); or (2) a constitutional convention, where the results are approved by ¾ of the states. I call this a purported supermajority because an amendment does not necessarily require a supermajority of *voters* to pass, but instead a supermajority of *states*. Due to the uneven distribution of population among the states, this leads to the prospect of a small minority of Americans who could effectively amend the Constitution. Not ideal, to say the least.

A Constitution is meant to be a special document that is above the fray of day-to-day politics, and to uphold the rights of 100% of the people. We must ensure that the document is flexible enough to allow for change when it becomes necessary from time to time. But making such changes should require enough of a consensus among the people, that is, a supermajority, to try to prevent clearly bad ideas from becoming entrenched.

An easy way to update the amendment process is to just strike the word "states" and put in "population of the United States." Easy fix. You're welcome.

"The object in life is not to be on the side of the majority, but to escape finding oneself in the ranks of the insane."

– Marcus Aurelius

Except that no system is fool proof. And sometimes many of us act like fools. In 1919, the 18th Amendment went into effect, prohibiting all manufacture or sale of alcohol within the United States, an era known as **Prohibition**. The amendment had the support of about 65% of Congress (due to several members abstaining, they reached the required 2/3 threshold), and all but 2 of the states. Of all the state legislators in the country, about 80% of them voted in favor of the amendment.[33]

For the sake of this argument, let's take the votes of the state legislators to be a direct channeling of the wishes of the population. You could say that the vast majority of the people supported the amendment. Assuming this is true, then even with a high supermajority requirement, the "wrong" things can still end up in the Constitution.

Thankfully, this period of Prohibition finally ended, and the Cincos de Mayo resumed, when the 18th Amendment was repealed in 1933. But this "system correction" took 14 long, dry years to occur. And you thought "dry January" was hard.

If this dumb law could be enshrined in the Constitution, what else could be? While we can and should have the proper structures in place to allow for better outcomes, we cannot rely on the system alone. It must be combined with a culture of critical thinking and deliberation.

On the whole, we should be skeptical of putting too much power in the hands of any single institution or group, including ourselves. We must have more humility, and we must remember that everyone has a different perspective on life (not that all perspectives are equally valid, particularly those based on hate). Everything the government does affects 100% of us, whether directly or indirectly. Let's be cautious with what some of the people impose on all the people. Maybe there can be a warning label on voting ballots that reminds us of this. We are truly all in this together.

If enough of us can come together to push for a change, we should be able to implement it. But if there's not enough support for change, then maybe it shouldn't happen. Even the People need to be checked and balanced.

Which brings us back to the hierarchy of power in our society. Instead of a hierarchy, perhaps it's better to think of the power structure as a circle – the circle of life (*The Lion King* went deep).

Section 6: How Does it All Affect Me?

Actions Have Consequences

What are the consequences of violating a law?

There are a range of possible consequences, depending on which laws are violated. Laws are classified as **criminal** or **civil**. Criminal laws generally involve more severe punishment, such as fines or jail time, and can only be enforced by the government. Civil laws generally call for less severe punishment, not involving jail time, and are enforced by private citizens and/or the government through a lawsuit.

To convict someone of criminal charges, the prosecution must prove that the defendant is guilty **beyond a reasonable doubt**, a very high standard that asks us to be quite sure of guilt before we deprive someone of their liberty or even life. Whereas, for a court to find that a defendant violated civil law, the must be proven by a **preponderance of the evidence**, usually interpreted as "more likely than not." The difference between the two is like "Oh, he's *super* guilty" vs "Ya, she probably did it."

If someone violates a **civil** law, usually the violator (**defendant**) can be sued in court and made to pay an amount of money to the violated person (**plaintiff**) to compensate them (called **money damages**). It is not always easy to determine what this amount should be, as many civil laws do not specify the specific consequences. Instead, it's left to the plaintiff to suggest a number to a judge and/or jury.

In addition, the plaintiff may be able to get the court to order the defendant to do something or refrain from doing something. This is called an **injunction**, and it is usually more challenging to obtain than money damages.

If someone violates a **criminal** law, usually the particular law specifies the maximum punishment, while the specific **sentence** is determined by the judge and/or jury in each case. Criminal laws are generally classified as **felonies**, **misdemeanors**, or even **infractions**.

Felonies are the most serious, and generally involve punishment in jail of greater than one year, plus fines, and may even include the death penalty in some states (see our online Guide to the Death Penalty). Misdemeanors are less serious, and involve jailtime of less than one year and/or paying a fine. Infractions are the most minor, and may involve small fines or a requirement to do a certain number of hours of **community service**, like picking up trash.

A person's actions can violate both civil and criminal law. Such a person could face both a lawsuit by the harmed persons, and criminal prosecution by the government.

Can a person be prosecuted or sued many years after the fact?

If enough time passes after the actions, or after *discovery* of the actions, there may be no consequences at all. Most laws have an "expiration date" for enforcement, called the **statute of limitations**. For example, if your consumer rights have been violated, you must sue the company within a certain number of years (usually 2-4 years). But, generally, the clock does not start ticking until you have discovered (or reasonably should have discovered) the issue.

Both civil and criminal laws have statutes of limitations. If a person is not prosecuted for a crime within a certain number of years, they cannot be punished! The major exception: murder. There's no rest for wicked murderers.

The reason to have time limits for enforcement of laws is that over time, certain forms of evidence may be lost, and memories fade. These rules are also intended to promote speedy and efficient justice.

If I happen to break a law that I wasn't aware of, can I say I didn't know about it to get off the hook?

Generally, no. Ignorance is usually not a valid defense to violating the law, unless the particular law itself requires that a person knew about the law and violated it anyway. For the most part, as crazy as it seems, you are actually expected to know pretty much ALL of the laws that apply to you.

If a person plans or attempts to commit a crime and fails, can they still be convicted of a crime?

Yes. There is no "no harm, no foul" rule in criminal law. Attempts to commit a criminal act, even if unsuccessful, are usually considered the same as if the crime was carried out.

Planning to commit a crime, without taking further steps, is somewhat different, however. This is known as **conspiracy** to commit a crime, and may involve a somewhat lesser punishment than actually committing the crime.

If there is no law against something, is it legal?

Maybe. In terms of criminal law, there is the concept that to prosecute someone for a crime, the acts in question must be clearly prohibited in the law. Otherwise the law or prosecution action can be thrown out as **void for vagueness**. And there is the Constitutional right that you cannot be criminally prosecuted for a crime that was not specifically illegal at the time you took the actions. That is, criminal laws cannot be **retroactive**.

However, this generally does not apply to *civil* laws (non-criminal). As for civil laws, even if certain conduct is not clearly prohibited at the time, a court could decide that the "spirit" of a law made that conduct illegal. Or that prior cases are similar enough to the conduct that the rulings in those cases should be extended to prohibit that conduct. Civil penalties may be applied retroactively.

Regardless of legality, it's important to not get caught up in the narrow question about whether an action is legal or constitutional. Just because something is not illegal, that does not mean it is right. We should also always consider whether our actions, and the actions of others, are moral and ethical.

Where Am I? (Jurisdictionally Speaking)

For most laws, your physical location at the time you take the action determines which laws apply and have **jurisdiction** over you. Let's say you are driving through the City of Los Angeles. You are subject to the laws of (1) the City of L.A., (local laws) (2) the state of California (state laws), and (3) the United States (federal laws). If you then drive through the city of Beverly Hills, you would be subject to that city's laws instead of L.A.'s laws.

Sometimes it can be tricky to determine what jurisdiction you are in at any point. If you are within an **incorporated city** or **municipality**, such as the city of Santa Monica, you are subject to that city's laws. But if you are in an **unincorporated area** such as Marina del Rey, CA, you are actually subject to the county laws, which are made by the Los Angeles County Board of Supervisors.

Sometimes people confuse their neighborhood or borough as being its own city. For example, if you live in the borough of Brooklyn, New York, your municipality is New York City, not Brooklyn; and your county is Kings County. Particularly troublesome is when a neighborhood has the word "city" in its name! Studio City, California: neither a studio nor a city (the municipality is the city of Los Angeles).

We have a tool on the Law Soup website to help you determine your municipality for just about any address in the country, which will help you find your local government and local laws. You can find it at: **Lawsoup.org/legal-basics**.

Even if you are not physically located in a certain location, you may also be subject to the laws of these other cities or states. This could happen if you own property in another state, or if you have a business that ships products to customers in another state.

If you are considered a **legal resident** of a city or state, you may be subject to certain laws, particularly tax laws, and rules about where you can sue and be sued. Legal residency or **domicile** can be determined differently for each relevant law. Most commonly, it is determined by such things as the address you put down on a form, or a place where you live at least 6 months of the year, or even a place where you *intend* to reside permanently.

Illegal Laws

Can a law be illegal?

Yes! It may sound odd, but a law can be considered illegal when it conflicts with a higher level law.

What happens if a law conflicts with another law?

In general, higher level laws override lower level laws. So, federal laws override state and local laws, and state laws override local laws. This is called **preemption**.

When there is a conflict of laws, it is usually a simple matter of a court applying the hierarchy of law. So, if a statute conflicts with the Constitution, then the Constitution overrides the statute, and the statute is **unconstitutional** and unenforceable.

However, if a lower level law is simply a stricter regulation than a higher level law, it is said there is no conflict, and the stricter regulation usually is effective. For example, federal minimum wage is $7.25 an hour (yes, it's really that low!). But many states and cities have higher minimum wage than that. So, employers in a city with a $15/hr minimum wage must pay $15/hr, and the federal minimum wage is essentially ignored.

On the next page is the hierarchy of laws, from highest level to lowest level. Note that common law (made by judges) and contractual obligations are generally superseded by statutes and other laws made by the legislative and executive branches.

CONFLICT OF LAWS: WHICH LAWS WIN?

FEDERAL
- U.S. CONSTITUTION
- FEDERAL STATUTES
- FEDERAL REGULATIONS

↓

STATE
- STATE CONSTITUTION
- STATE STATUTES
- STATE REGULATIONS

↓

LOCAL
- CITY CHARTER
- LOCAL ORDINANCES
- LOCAL REGULATIONS

↓

- COMMON LAW
- CONTRACT LAW

What about international law?

You may note that in the hierarchy of laws there is no mention of **international law**. There is no true world government which can create and enforce global laws. The **United Nations** (UN) is an organization designed to facilitate relations among the various nations of the world. Yet each country maintains its **sovereignty**, meaning the full right and power to govern itself.

International laws, such as **treaties** with other countries, and the creation of **international courts**, are generally not self-executing. This means that in order to give effect to international law, Congress must pass federal statutes to implement these international laws.

Do I have to follow a law that I know is illegal?

Generally, yes. You can challenge the law and sue to overturn it, but while doing so you still must follow the law! However, there is an exception for extreme situations: if a law or order violates human rights and you believe it will later be determined as such by a court, you should not follow it. Those who follow such laws cannot claim they were "just following orders." The Nazi soldiers who used this excuse were still punished severely during the Nuremberg trials.

If you have already violated a law, and you are being sued or prosecuted for it, you may claim in your defense that the law is illegal. The court may or may not implement a **stay** or hold on the proceedings against you, while it determines whether the law is valid or not. If the court ultimately finds that the law is invalid, you will be relieved of any punishment or other consequences.

It's All a Process

If you ever plan to get sued or charged with a crime, or you just feel like suing someone today, here's what you need to know about the process of **civil litigation** (lawsuits) and **criminal prosecution**. Note that the specific steps and terminology may vary by state and locality, but the general process usually works similarly.

What is the process of a civil lawsuit?

Civil lawsuits usually involve multiple steps, stretching at least months and often years. This can cost thousands of dollars in court fees alone, and tens of thousands in legal fees. But don't be discouraged by these figures, as there are ways of pursuing this process without paying upfront. See Article 4 for more on this.

Here's the typical process:

Step 1: Demands & Negotiations

Let's say you hire a company to do some renovation work on your house. Unfortunately, they botched the job; it looks terrible, and you want them to fix it or get some money back. First, try to work it out directly with the other party. This may begin with a **demand letter** in which you clearly state exactly what you want from the other party (usually a dollar amount and/or specific actions for them to take).

You may be able to come to a **settlement**, in which possibly a dollar amount is paid out and you would not need to continue legal proceedings. Note that if the settlement doesn't come together at this stage, it can still happen at any time throughout the process.

Step 2: File Lawsuit

If the other party refuses your demands, the next step may be to file a lawsuit. To get a lawsuit started, you, the **plaintiff**, would submit paperwork, the **complaint**, to a court. You must also provide proper **notice** to the other party, the **defendant**, that they have been sued.

To give proper notice, you can't just text the defendant saying "see you in court, buddy." You must have someone hand the papers to the defendant IRL (in person). This is called **serving** the defendant, or giving them **service of process**. The person who does this is called, appropriately, a **process server**.

The defendant must then file a response with the court, called an **answer**, admitting or denying the various claims. They also have the opportunity to **countersue** you if they feel they have claims against you (be careful what you *sue* for).

If the defendant never responds to the lawsuit, the plaintiff may be awarded an automatic win, called a **default judgment**.

Step 3: Discovery

Sounds exciting, right? Like an Indiana Jones adventure or something. And it certainly can be, if you find a "smoking gun" piece of evidence. But usually it involves lawyers poring over thousands of documents, probably not finding very many gold nuggets. In this phase, each party can request information and documents from the other party, and each is generally required to provide what is requested (although much of the time the parties push back hard on these requests, for various legitimate and not so legitimate reasons). This may involve written questions or requests for documents. It may also involve **depositions**, which is where one party asks the other to come in for an interview.

Depositions are similar to questioning a witness in court, as they are usually taken under penalty of **perjury**. This means that if the respondent is later found to have lied during the deposition, they can be prosecuted for it. The main difference is, instead of court they often take place in a conference room of a law office, and are more informal.

Step 4: Pre-Trial

If one side believes that the evidence uncovered during discovery is enough to win the case without going to trial, they may ask the judge (make a **motion**) to grant **summary judgment**. If the judge grants summary judgment, this means he or she believes the trial could not possibly provide additional useful information, so it would be a waste of time. Therefore, the judge issues a **judgment**, which generally ends the case, unless it is appealed.

After discovering whatever it is the parties are trying to discover about each other, the parties often go through **mediation** to try to settle before going to trial. This involves working with a neutral third-party **mediator** to try to come to an agreement and end the fight. Often the court will make this step mandatory, but not always. Mediation can also occur at any point before or during the litigation.

Step 5: Trial

Trials may involve a **jury**, a group of citizens selected to consider the evidence presented by both sides. Based on this **fact-finding**, the jury determines whether the law was violated or not. Other times, the parties prefer to have the judge act as the jury, in what is called a **bench trial**. In fact, less than 1% of cases use a jury!

Step 6: Judgment

At some point after the trial, the judge will issue his or her **judgment** as to who wins and who loses. If it was a jury trial, the judge will usually rely on the jury's findings. Sometimes the judge may reduce the compensation the jury **awarded** to the plaintiff if it is excessive. The judgment is a binding **legal opinion**, which usually involves an **order** for the parties to do something, such as for the defendant to give the plaintiff money, or a **declaration**, such as that the defendant is not liable for the alleged legal violations.

Step 7: Appeal

Usually the loser will have the opportunity to **appeal** the judgment to a higher court. The appeals court opinion could in turn be appealed to an even higher court. In a case involving state law, the end of the line is usually the state supreme court, unless there are any federal issues, in which case it could GO.ALL.THE.WAY.TO... the U.S. Supreme Court, which could be... fun? Alas, this is extremely unlikely, since, as you know now, the Supreme Court takes less than 2% of the cases requested.

Step 8: Enforce Judgment

After all appeals have been said and done, aka **exhausted** (everyone involved in the lawsuit is probably exhausted at that point), it is time for the loser to do what the court ordered. Usually this means it's time to pay up. But what happens if the loser just doesn't? The courts generally do not enforce judgments on their own. You may need to take various enforcement actions, including requesting the court to declare the loser in **contempt of court**. Then you could get law enforcement involved to seize the loser's assets.

Are there any alternatives to the civil process?

Yes. If the dollar amount you are suing for is small, around $10,000 or so (varies based on state), you can sue in **small claims court**. This is usually a much shorter, more informal process that does not have as many rules as a standard lawsuit. Also, there is **arbitration**, which is a dispute resolution process outside the court system entirely. This is also generally quicker and less formal than a typical lawsuit.

What is the process of a criminal prosecution?

Step 1: Arrest

A person may be arrested if law enforcement has **probable cause** to believe they have committed a crime (more on this later). At this point or any point in the process, the suspect and prosecution may agree to a **plea deal**. This is where the suspect agrees to plead guilty in order to serve a lesser punishment than they might if the prosecution continued.

Step 2: Charges Filed (Indictment)

Generally, the suspect can only be held for up to 48 hours before law enforcement brings formal charges (called the **indictment** or **information**).

Step 3: Trial

In criminal cases, the defendant has the right to a jury trial when charged with a serious crime (more on that later). But many defendants prefer to take their chances with a judge rather than a jury of citizens who may be even *more* "judgmental." The prosecution provides evidence of the **defendant**'s alleged crimes, and the judge or jury determines guilt or innocence.

Step 4: Judgment

The jury (if there is one) provides its **verdict**, and the judge usually issues his or her judgment based on this verdict. However, sometimes the judge may **set aside the verdict** or declare a **mistrial** if something improper occurred.

Step 5: Sentencing

The judge determines how much of a fine and/or jail time to impose, based on the range allowed by the crimes at issue.

Step 6: Appeal

Usually only the defendant may appeal, not the prosecution. So if you win at trial, you're free! What are you going to do now? (Please, don't say you're going to Disneyland.)

How Appealing

How do appeals work?

It is said that everyone gets their day in court. But also, everyone gets at least a "second bite at the apple." Depending on the case, you may even get 3 or 4 bites at the apple.

Do judges ever get the law wrong?

Yes and no. Yes, meaning they are human, so of course they make mistakes or errors in judgment. This is what appeals are for: a higher court tells the lower court it was wrong. But it's all essentially opinions, and opinions can never be "right" or "wrong." The law is simply what courts say it is. Until the next court says it is something else.

That said, the opinions must be based on facts. Sometimes cases can be overturned, even years later, when new facts come to light. This often happens with DNA evidence that clearly shows a person was wrongly convicted. In these situations, usually the case can be reopened, and the judgment can be overturned. If a wrongly convicted person has served jail time, they will normally get financial compensation from the government. If they have been executed, well, unfortunately there's no way to undo that yet. A good reason to get rid of the death penalty.

What happens if I win in court?

If you win, the other party may be able to appeal the ruling to a higher court. If they don't appeal, your win is finalized, and you just need to make sure the judgment is enforced. This is sometimes easier said than done (see Article 4: How do I exercise my rights?).

What happens if I lose in court?

If you lose in the first level court, you can appeal the ruling to the appeals court. That appeals court can then decide whether the lower court got it "right" or "wrong." If it says the lower court was *right*, then the lower court ruling goes into effect, and you still lose. Unless you are able to appeal to the supreme court. If the appeals court says the lower court was *wrong*, then that ruling is overturned, and you win. Unless the other party is able to appeal to the supreme court.

Remember that the supreme court doesn't have to take the case. But if it does, it can either affirm or overturn the appeals court.

If everyone knows someone is guilty of a crime, why bother with a trial?

Many people believe that "bad people," like suspected terrorists, mafia and gang members, etc. don't "deserve" fair and proper treatment, such as a fair trial and legal representation. "They didn't treat their victims fairly, so why should we do that for them?"

But that's not the right way to look at it. It's not so much about that particular suspect, but rather, when these rights are upheld consistently, *everyone's* rights are strengthened. If we start making exceptions for this person or these types of people, then soon these rights will erode over time. Law enforcement may begin to not worry about protecting *anyone's* rights.

> *"The rights of every man are diminished when the rights of one man are threatened."*
>
> *— John F. Kennedy*

There are also numerous cases in which the evidence shows that, although a suspect may be "suspect," he is actually not guilty. Police definitely do not always get it right. Not only that, but, as previously discussed, sometimes even after a person is convicted of a crime, evidence comes to light later on which clearly shows they were not guilty. These issues are why the concepts of Due Process and Rule of Law are so important, and affect all of us.

Section 7: Let's Get Real

Now that we have discussed how things are supposed to work, let's talk about how it works in the real world.

If the law is on my side, will I get justice?

Let's get real: Although the law may be on your side in a particular situation, there's often no good remedy available. For example, if you order some products from a company and they send you the wrong things, which causes you a minor inconvenience, you probably can't get anything out of it other than your money back. This is because your "harm" suffered was minor, so a court would not easily be able to assign a dollar amount to it. Thus the court could not order the company to do anything to compensate.

But even if there is a significant dollar amount involved, and you *do* get a judgment in your favor, you still may not see a payout. Sometimes the company or individual you are suing simply doesn't have the money to pay the judgment. As they say, you can't get blood from a stone.

What are my options if someone does something illegal to me?

As we discussed, there are different consequences depending on whether someone violates a criminal law or civil law. If someone commits a crime against you, call 9-1-1 if it is ongoing or just occurred, or call or visit your local police station to report it and **press charges**. If the police and prosecutor's office believe there is sufficient evidence to prosecute the offender for crime(s), they will do so, and the offender may end up in jail.

If someone commits an offense against you that is a violation of civil law, you can sue them in court for **money damages** to compensate for the harms to you. Yes, it's damages for the damage. You may also be able to get a court to order the offender to do something or refrain from doing something, which is called an **injunction**.

Some offenses can be both civil and criminal. For example, if someone punches you in the face, this is likely considered the *crime* of battery, as well as a *civil* battery. You can file a complaint with the police, who may then prosecute the assailant. The assailant could then end up in jail. In addition, you can sue the assailant in civil court for money damages.

What are options for less significant harms?

For certain "minor" harms suffered, there is a mechanism which enables many people to combine similar claims, making it more feasible to get a remedy. This is called a **class action**. It is often used for consumer or employer issues. You have almost certainly been part of a class action at some point, whether you realize it or not. You know all those data breaches in which a company gets hacked and your personal information is stolen? You're probably not going to sue over that on your own.

But when a few of the affected people get together and sue in a class action, they can get compensation for *all* of the (potentially millions) of affected people. If the lawsuit is successful, the ones who actually pursue the legal action usually get more money than the passive plaintiffs. The passive plaintiffs may not get much – maybe $10, maybe $100 – but the process of claiming your small piece of the pie is generally as simple as filling out a short form.

There is also **small claims court**, which is for claims of up to around $5,000-$10,000, depending on the state. In some states the limit is $25,000. Definitely not a small amount for many people, but at these dollar amounts, it is often not worth it to hire a lawyer to take the case. Small claims court is designed for non-lawyers to be able to handle themselves. However, it still can be somewhat complicated and involves a significant amount of time and effort. And of course, you need to know the law.

It is usually a good idea to at least consult with a lawyer for a couple hours or more. There is a common misconception here. It is true that many states do not allow lawyers to *represent* clients in small claims court (because it's designed to level the playing field), meaning the lawyer can't show up to the hearing on your behalf. That said, you can always *consult* with a lawyer before or after the hearing.

Can I sue someone for being a jerk?

No, probably not, if it doesn't involve illegal discrimination or otherwise violates your rights. There is no law against being mean. But if someone makes a serious threat to harm you, and takes any steps towards that, you could possibly sue or have them arrested for **assault**. Or if someone severely harms you emotionally and you end up going to therapy or getting on psychiatric medication, you may be able to successfully sue for **intentional infliction of emotional distress**.

I'm not sure what the law says but I was definitely wronged. Can't I just explain my story to a judge?

Let's say your enemy, Nemesis, did some generalized evil to you. Like many people, you may think, if you can just get in front of a judge (or jury) and tell the judge how terrible Nemesis is, and what he did to you, the judge will empathize with you and throw the book at Nemesis. But it doesn't work that way. Judges are not all-powerful, deciding right from wrong simply as they see fit. Court decisions must generally be based on specific preexisting laws and rules.

Laws are not always logical (they are made by humans after all), and they are not always simply about doing the right thing. Even if a judge doesn't believe the law is fair, she or he still must (generally) follow it, and decide the case accordingly. The judge may hate Nemesis too. But it's not their job to act on these feelings.

That said, there is a caveat (isn't there always). The full picture is that sometimes judges (or juries) are expressly allowed to consider fairness or **equity** when the relevant law calls for a **balancing** of various factors to determine the outcome of a case. Even when they are not explicitly allowed to do so, many if not most judges and juries do consciously or subconsciously consider fairness when deciding a case. But they always must express their opinion on the basis of some preexisting law(s). When juries do it, it's referred to as **jury nullification**.

Help! I'm being sued (or threatened with a lawsuit)!

If you received a notice of a lawsuit against you, often called a **summons**, stay calm. It might not a big deal. But you should almost certainly consult with a lawyer ASAP. Whatever you do, don't ignore the summons. As discussed earlier, if a person being sued doesn't respond and doesn't show up to court, the court can issue a default judgment against them.

Keep in mind that the person suing you would almost certainly prefer not to go through the whole trial and all, so try to negotiate and work out a settlement. And if someone has only threatened to sue, but hasn't filed anything, they may not actually intend to do so. A lawyer can help sort it out.

Article 3:
What Rights (and Duties) Do I Have?

Article 3: What Rights (and Duties) Do I Have?

We've talked about the history, the systems and the processes. But you probably want to know some specifics, right? What exactly is legal and illegal? In this part of the book, we get into all of that. Well, not all of that. Remember how there's thousands of laws? We can't cover all of them.

Here's some of the most important. These include civil rights, such as free speech, privacy rights, rights when interacting with police, rights as a victim of crime; as well as property rights, tenant rights, and contract basics. But there are other areas you may want to know about, such as your rights as a consumer or employee, or laws about injuries, harassment, healthcare, the environment, taxes, business, internet, etc. You can find these and more at the Law Soup website.

I mentioned some disclaimers in the Preamble, but these are especially relevant in this part: Laws change frequently, so some of this information may be out of date by the time you are reading this. For the most up to date info, check the Law Soup website or consult with a lawyer. And again, I must give my standard disclaimer: the information here is not legal advice and is not intended to substitute for consulting with a lawyer.

Section 1: What are My Civil Rights?

When people talk about **civil rights**, **individual rights**, or **political rights**, this generally includes fundamental rights we have as individuals to participate in society as equals and with dignity. More specifically, it includes freedom of expression, free exercise of religion, voting rights, rights against law enforcement overreach, "innocent until proven guilty," rights against unfair discrimination, among others.

Many of these rights come from the **Bill of Rights** (first 10 amendments to the U.S. Constitution), other parts of the Constitution, state constitutions, as well as laws passed by Congress and the states. Here are the various types of civil rights and what is protected.

Free Speech and Expression

Free speech is one of the most important rights, as all other rights depend on people being able to speak out about them to ensure they are respected. Under the 1st Amendment of the U.S. Constitution, you have broad rights to speak freely, especially regarding politics. See the full guide to free speech, below.

Religious Rights

The 1st amendment also grants the right to freely exercise religion. Under this amendment, the government may not impose any religion upon you, and the government may not be entangled with religion. This is known as a **wall of separation between church and state**. As an example, it is unconstitutional for a public school to impose prayer and other religious practices on students.

Rights Against Law Enforcement Overreach

Under the 4th amendment of the U.S. Constitution, you have the right against the government performing unreasonable searches of you and unreasonable taking of your property. See our guide to interacting with the police, below.

"Innocent Until Proven Guilty"

This is part of the right to **due process of law**. Under the 5th amendment, the government may not take certain actions against you, such as keeping you in jail, until they prove in a fair and independent judicial proceeding that you have committed a crime.

To ensure that the process against you is fair, you have certain specific rights. This includes the right to be provided a defense attorney free of charge, if you can't afford one and either you are currently in jail or the crime carries a potential penalty of more than 1 year (a **felony**).[34] You also have a right to a jury trial (6th amendment) for crimes which carry a possible sentence of more than 6 months in jail.[35] Third, you have the right to not have to say things that may incriminate you (5th amendment).

What can I do if someone calls the police on me but I didn't do anything wrong?

If a private citizen calls the police on you, knowing that you did not commit any crimes, you may be able to successfully sue that person for **malicious prosecution**. This is also sometimes called **abuse of process** or **abuse of civil process** or **wrongful use of civil proceedings**.

No Cruel and Unusual Punishment

Under the 8th amendment, you have the right not to be subjected to **"cruel and unusual punishment."** The Supreme Court's interpretation of this phrase has evolved over the years, from prohibiting what is clearly torture, to now banning the death penalty for individuals who are under the age of 18 or have an intellectual disability. See more on this at our online Guide to the Death Penalty.

Who Gets to Be a Citizen?

Under the 14th amendment, every person born on U.S. soil is a citizen of the United States. Others may be eligible to become citizens through a process known as **naturalization**. These rules are provided in the Immigration and Nationality Act, and other immigration laws.

Can the government strip citizenship from someone?

The government generally may not strip citizenship (aka **denaturalize**) from any person, except in very limited circumstances. One such circumstance is **treason**, which involves acts of severe harm to the government.

Do immigrants or non-citizens have rights?

Yes, most civil rights apply to every individual in the country, whether they are here legally or not. But there are some important differences. See our online Guide to Laws about Immigration & Travel to the U.S.

Who Gets to Vote?

Every American citizen at least 18 years old and who has not been convicted of a felony (although some states allow felons to vote) is eligible to vote. See more about voting rights at our online Guide to Voting Laws.

Equality & Discrimination

In general, individuals in the U.S. are protected from many, but not necessarily all, forms of discrimination, on the basis of race, religion, gender, sexual orientation, disability and certain other characteristics. This is based on the U.S. Constitution, particularly the equal protection clause of 14th amendment. It is also based on the Civil Rights Act, and other federal laws. Many states go further and provide even stronger protections than the federal government.

"We're a nation that says give us your tired, your poor, your huddled masses yearning to breathe free. A nation built on our differences, guided by the belief that we're all created equal."

– Michelle Obama

Is racial discrimination always illegal?

Unequal treatment of people based on race is illegal in many circumstances. In general, under the 14th Amendment, the government may not discriminate on the basis of race. Under the Civil Rights Act, employers may not take any discriminatory actions against employees or prospective employees on the basis of their race. Restaurants, shops, etc. cannot refuse to serve people on the basis of their race.

Is gender discrimination illegal?

Unequal treatment of people based on their gender or sex is illegal in certain circumstances. In general, the government may not discriminate on the basis of gender or sex. Employers may not take any discriminatory actions against employees or prospective employees on the basis of their gender or sex.

Is it illegal to discriminate on the basis of sexual orientation or gender identity (LGBT people)?

Unequal treatment of lesbian, gay, bisexual, transgender, or other sexual and gender identities is illegal in certain circumstances. In general, the government may not discriminate on the basis of sexual orientation. Same sex couples have the right to be married in any state in the U.S.

Employers may not take any discriminatory actions against employees or prospective employees on the basis of their sexual or gender identity.[36]

Is it illegal to discriminate against someone because of their religion?

The government is limited in its ability to discriminate on the basis of religion, under the 1st amendment of the U.S. Constitution. Employers and businesses are also limited in their ability to discriminate on this basis.

Is it illegal to discriminate against someone because of a disability?

The government and businesses must make certain accommodations for individuals with a disability, under the Americans with Disabilities Act.

Reproductive Rights

Is there a right to abortion?

As of June 2022, there is no nationwide right to abortion. Each state has its own abortion laws. Some states ban abortion entirely, while others allow it up to around 6 months after conception.

Prior to June 2022, the law was that, at a minimum, women have the right to an abortion up until the point when the fetus becomes **viable** (able to survive outside the womb), which is usually about 6 months after conception. And the law held that a woman may have an abortion at *any time*, even after viability, if necessary for her life or health.

These rights were based on the important Supreme Court cases of **Roe v Wade** (1973) and **Planned Parenthood v Casey** (1992), which were decided by applying the due process clause in the 14th amendment of the U.S. Constitution. Yet rather than the traditional due process question of fair procedures, these cases were based on a concept called **substantive due process**. This is the idea that the government may not deprive anyone of "life, liberty, or property" without adequate justification, regardless of the procedural fairness.

These decisions were overturned by the Supreme Court in Dobbs v. Jackson Women's Health Organization (2022), which held that abortion is not included in the 14th amendment's conception of "liberty." The court said abortion was not a "deeply rooted" right in the nation's history.

Can the government ban or restrict access to contraception?

No. Contraception is protected by the due process clause under the concept of substantive due process.[37]

Right to Own Guns for Self-defense

Under the 2nd amendment, you have the right to own some types of guns for self-defense purposes, subject to certain limitations. Fully automatic weapons are prohibited throughout the country. Many states also restrict semi-automatic firearms. See our online Guide to Weapons Law.

Section 2: What are My Rights in Interacting with the Police?

This is a guide to your rights regarding law enforcement actions in the United States. Here are the most important laws you need to know about interacting with the police, police conduct and police misconduct. These rules on **police**

work generally apply to all levels of law enforcement, including FBI, NSA, your local police, etc. However, your state may provide additional protections against law enforcement overreach.

Laws regarding police conduct are very complex, involve many specific rules, and change frequently. If you feel that your rights have been violated, we strongly urge you to find a lawyer who specializes in criminal and constitutional law.

Due Process & the Police

Due process means the government, including law enforcement, must follow proper and fair procedures when enforcing the law against an individual, or when otherwise taking an action that could deprive a person of "life, liberty, or property." This comes from the U.S. Constitution, 5th and 14th Amendments.

It means that the police cannot search, arrest, use force against, or take things from people without justification. Law enforcement must carefully and respectfully collect evidence of crimes, to be used later in a fair and impartial court proceeding against alleged perpetrators. If they fail to uphold these standards, officers can be severely punished, including receiving time in jail. But generally they are given wide latitude in carrying out their dangerous and challenging duties.

"The police must obey the law while enforcing the law."

- Earl Warren, Supreme Court Justice

Confrontations with Police

Do I have the right to take video of police?

Yes. You have the right to take video or photos of police officers in public spaces, and the police may NOT interfere with your recording. But you may not physically obstruct police work.[38]

Is it illegal to be rude to the police, or say or do offensive things to them?

In general, no it's not illegal to do this (although you will likely get more unwanted attention from the officers by doing so). One case involved a police officer who gave a woman a more serious violation simply because she "flipped him off" (gave him the middle finger). The courts ruled that the officer had no right to do so, as her actions were protected by the 1st amendment.[39] See more about free speech, below.

Are police allowed to kick me off the sidewalk?

As long as you are not blocking the flow of traffic, you generally have the right to be on a public sidewalk or to peacefully gather with others on public sidewalks. Police may not unreasonably restrict this right.[40] To march or assemble on the *streets* or *roads*, you will usually need to get a permit with the city.

Searches

Can police search me any time they want?

No. You have the right to be free from "unreasonable" searches by the government/police of your body or anything you are wearing, your car, your home, and some other personal areas.[41] This essentially means that before law enforcement is allowed to search you, they must believe it is more likely than not that you have committed some crime and that evidence of that crime will be found in the search. The legal term for this is **probable cause**. But keep in mind, a "pat down" is not considered a "search" (see below).

If the police have probable cause to believe you committed a crime or they will find evidence of a crime, then they *generally* (exceptions below) must get a **warrant** in order to conduct a search.

How does a police officer obtain a warrant?

A police officer obtains a **search warrant** by convincing a judge that he or she will likely find evidence of a crime in searching you.

When does a police officer need a warrant to search me?

In general, police must have a search warrant to search you, but there are many exceptions to this requirement. Specifically, some of the situations police are allowed to search you *without* getting a warrant include:

- any kind of surveillance that an average citizen could do, using any technology that an average citizen could possess[42]
- searching (and taking) your garbage, once you put it on the sidewalk or street[43]
- a police dog sniffing you[44]
- a radio transmitter or "beeper" that monitors someone's movement along public roads[45] (but not in private areas, and not a GPS tracker – see below)
- where you do NOT have a **reasonable expectation of privacy**. This means the police can generally view and take photos or video of you or anything you do in public, or anything which is visible from a place where law enforcement is legally allowed to be, such as the street or sidewalk[46]
- "emergency" circumstances, such as when the police believe it is imminent that you are committing or will

commit a crime or destroy evidence; or to protect the health and safety of others[47]

- **"stop and frisk"** (see below)

Some of the situations police MUST get a warrant before searching you include the following (but these generally don't apply in emergencies):

- any kind of surveillance that an average citizen could NOT do, including use any technology that an average citizen could NOT possess, such as thermal imaging[48]
- a radio transmitter or "beeper" that tracks your movements in *private* areas, such as your home[49]
- installing a GPS tracking device on a car to monitor the vehicle's movements[50]
- Searching the contents of your cellphone or computer, even if you are arrested, and even at a U.S. border crossing.[51] Note that a court may require you to give your fingerprint to unlock a device, but courts may NOT require you to give up a password or passcode.
- Obtaining your cell phone location data from your mobile phone carrier[52]
- Searching your car (but if you are lawfully arrested, police may search the car, but MUST get a warrant to search the trunk)[53]
- Hotel guest records[54]

Seizures: When can the police take my property?

You have the right to be free from "unreasonable" taking of your property by the government/police. This means that before law enforcement can take or **seize** your property, they must believe it is more likely than not that you are committing or have committed a crime involving the property. In general, police must have a warrant to seize property. But there are many exceptions, including if evidence of a crime is clearly visible (for example, drugs), or for public safety reasons.[55]

There is also the controversial practice of **civil asset forfeiture**, in which the police may seize a person's assets, without needing to charge the person with any crimes. This kind of seizure may *give* you a seizure! This can occur if they believe that the *assets* themselves have been involved in a crime. But this practice of confiscating property is limited by the Constitutional protection against "excessive fines."[56] And many states have begun constraining this practice.

Arrests

Can the police arrest me whenever they want?

You have the right to be free from "unreasonable" arrests by the police. This means that before law enforcement can arrest or **seize** you, they must have a reasonable belief that it is more likely than not that you are committing or have committed a crime.

If the police violate this standard, it is often considered **false arrest** or **false imprisonment**. In general, police must have an **arrest warrant** to arrest you *within your home*, with some exceptions. Police do NOT need an arrest warrant to arrest you *in public*.[57]

What is stop and frisk and is it legal?

Stop and frisk occurs when the police stop you briefly and pat you down for weapons or evidence of a crime. This is sometimes called a **Terry pat** or **Terry stop**, based on the case of *Terry v. Ohio*.[58] Stop and frisk is not legally considered either a search or arrest, but it does fall within the 4th amendment.

Because it is considered less intrusive than a full search or arrest, police do not need probable cause. They only need **reasonable suspicion** that crime is afoot to be able to stop you and pat you down. A recent court case in New York held that the NYPD's stop and frisk practices were unconstitutional, as they were directed disproportionately towards certain racial or ethnic groups without the required level of reasonable suspicion.[59]

What are my rights if I am arrested?

If you have ever seen a police drama movie or show, these will sound familiar. Upon being arrested, you have the following rights, usually referred to as **Miranda rights**:[60]

- Right to remain silent when the police ask you questions (because you do not have to incriminate yourself).

- Right to an attorney. If you cannot afford an attorney, the government will provide one free of charge.
- After an arrest, if police don't formally charge you with a crime within a short period of time, they must release you.
- **Miranda warning**: Upon arresting you, police (usually) must explain these rights to you.

A little trivia: Miranda rights were established in 1966 when the Supreme Court decided the case of *Miranda v. Arizona*. The Court ruled that the police violated the 5th and 6th amendment rights of Ernesto Miranda, who was nonetheless convicted of some pretty heinous crimes which I would rather not mention here.

Do the police have to announce the reason for arrest at the time of the arrest?

It depends on the state. Unless your state has a specific law, police officers do *not* necessarily need to announce the reason for arrest.[61]

BUT a person arrested must be given a **probable cause hearing**, ordinarily within 48 hours of their arrest. The government will have to inform the suspect of the reason for arrest at that time, as the government has to establish probable cause based on a specific offense.[62]

Can the government hold someone indefinitely?

If you are legally present in the U.S., it is illegal and unconstitutional for the government to detain you against your will for a lengthy or undetermined period of time (usually must be within 48 hours) without going through the proper criminal justice process. This is called **indefinite detention** and is a violation of the rights of **due process of law** (sometimes just called **due process**).[63] But the law is different for people in the U.S. without authorization. See our online guide to laws about immigration & travel to the U.S.

Excessive Force

Is it illegal for the police to harass me or "rough me up"?

In general, law enforcement may not use physical force against another unless necessary. The use of force is justified only in limited circumstances, such as to compel someone to submit to a lawful arrest, or for self-defense or to defend others. If police violate this standard it may be considered a federal crime. You could also potentially sue the officer and the police agency where the officer works.[64] This is sometimes called **abuse of power** or **abuse of discretion**.

When are police shootings illegal?

When a police officer shoots someone, it may or may not be considered **excessive force**. It's usually up to the jury to decide whether the officer acted **reasonably** under the circumstances. But in general, officers are entitled to

qualified immunity when they do not act in such a way that has been clearly stated as illegal in prior court cases.[65]

Lying to Police

Is it illegal to lie to police?

Yes, this is usually considered the crime of **obstruction of justice**. Or if the lie is made while **under oath** or **under penalty of perjury**, then it can be considered the crime of perjury.

Is it illegal to file a false police report?

Yes, it is a felony to lie to police and say something happened when it did not. Law enforcement can charge this as **filing a false report** or more generally, **disorderly conduct**, or both.

Section 3: What are My Rights If I Am a Victim of Crime?

If you or someone you know is a victim of a crime, or someone has threatened to harm you or otherwise commit a crime against you, you have the following rights in the U.S. If you are a victim of a crime under state or local law (which includes most crimes), your rights as a victim vary by state, but most states provide many of the same rights listed here. For specific resources and a how-to guide, see Article 4 on Pressing Charges.

Law Enforcement Duty to Investigate Crime and Protect Victims

Police have a responsibility to protect you from valid threats of crime, and investigate any valid reports of a crime. If they don't, you may be able to sue the police or have the federal government prosecute the police for failing to do their duty, especially if due to discrimination.

Victims' Rights Before Criminal Charges Filed

Under the Victims' Rights and Restitution Act (VRRA), if you are a victim of a crime under federal law or any crime committed in Washington, DC, you have the following rights:

- *Notice:* To be notified that you have been the victim of a federal crime;
- *Information about services:* To be informed of the place where you may receive medical and social services, counseling, treatment, and other support services;
- *Protection:* To receive reasonable protection from a suspected offender and persons acting together with the suspected offender;
- *Status*: To know the status of the investigation of the crime, to the extent it is appropriate and it will not interfere with the investigation;
- *Property*: To have personal property being held for evidentiary purposes maintained in good condition and returned as soon as it is no longer needed for evidentiary purposes.

Victims' Rights After Charges Filed

If federal charges are filed involving images or material depicting the victim, victims (or a parent, guardian, or other appropriate alternate contact while victim is a minor) will have the following rights:

- *Notice.* The right to reasonable, accurate, and timely notice of any public court proceeding, or any parole proceeding, involving the crime, or if the accused has been released or has escaped;

- *Attend hearings.* The right not to be excluded from any such public court proceeding, unless the court determines that your testimony would be influenced by things you may hear at the proceeding;

- *Right to be heard.* The right to be reasonably heard at any public proceeding in the district court involving release, plea, or sentencing, or any parole proceeding;

- *Confer with prosecution.* The reasonable right to confer with the attorney for the government in the case;

- *Compensation.* The right to full and timely return of any property stolen or compensation for damaged property if the specific law requires;

- *Speedy proceedings.* The right to proceedings free from unreasonable delay;

- *Respect.* The right to be treated with fairness and with respect for your dignity and privacy.

Hate Crimes

You have the right to protection against **hate crimes** where an attacker uses (or attempts to use) a deadly weapon and the attack was motivated by your actual or perceived race, religion, national origin, gender, sexual orientation, gender identity, or disability.

Deadlines for Prosecuting Assailant

Though it varies by state and by type of crime, there are usually deadlines for prosecuting a person for committing a crime. These deadlines are called the **statute of limitations**. For example, in many states, rape must be prosecuted within 10 years or the assailant will essentially get away with it. Murder is one of the few crimes which never has a deadline for prosecuting.

Section 4: What are My Free Speech Rights?

Freedom of speech and expression is one of the most important rights we have. If we are to protect and expand our other rights, we must be able to discuss these issues freely and without significant limitation. Free speech is protected mostly by the 1st amendment in the U.S. Constitution. But the 1st amendment doesn't protect ALL speech or expression. There are limits. And it only prevents the *government* from

What Rights (and Duties) Do I Have? 129

restricting speech. Private individuals or companies generally may limit or censor speech.

Protected Speech

What type of speech does the 1st amendment protect?

The government generally may NOT restrict any of the following, meaning you have the right to do these things (with some exceptions, discussed below):

- political speech, including on school campuses,[66] or using offensive language
- burning or refusing to salute the American flag
- refusing to speak
- using offensive language towards police
- speaking in a **public forum**
- alternative holiday displays
- contribute money to political campaigns (with limits)
- advertise products or services

Can the government restrict the right to protest or make political speech?

Generally, you have the right to protest or make political speech. Except that the government may require you to get a permit to assemble a group of people; may restrict noise levels; and may prevent you from trespassing on private property, and impose other similar restrictions. These are called **time, place, and manner** restrictions. Any such regulations or restrictions must NOT be based on the *content* of the speech, except when the content violates any of the rules below.

What about using offensive language for political purposes?

You have the right to use offensive language to convey a political message.[67] In 1968, Paul Cohen was at a Los Angeles courthouse, wearing a jacket that said "Fuck the Draft." He was arrested and convicted for **disturbing the peace**. The U.S. Supreme Court later ruled that he should not have been convicted of any crime, as he was properly exercising his free speech rights.

"Whoever would overthrow the liberty of a nation must begin by subduing the freeness of speech."

— Benjamin Franklin

Is it illegal to burn the American flag?

No. The government cannot prohibit burning or otherwise damaging or destroying the American flag.[68] While federal law contains a **U.S. Flag Code** dictating rules for handling the flag, and declaring that "no disrespect shall be shown" to the flag,[69] this is essentially advisory. These rules do not have the force of law, as they would be unconstitutional if enforced.

Is it illegal to refuse to salute or "honor" the American flag?

No. Generally you have the right to decide not to speak or express yourself. As an example, you have the right to refuse to salute the flag.[70] However, in certain circumstances the government may compel you to speak (see compelled speech below).

Is it illegal to use offensive language or gestures towards the police?

No. You generally have the right to use offensive language or gestures towards police, such as flipping off a police officer.[71] However, I do not recommend this.

Do I have the right to speak in public?

You have the right to speak in a **public forum** or **public square**, which is a physical or digital space that is deemed or understood to be a place for the public to discuss issues of importance.

Can the government block me from social media?

Social media accounts in which the government exerts some control or are used for any official business, such as a politician's twitter account, are considered a public forum. In these situations, the government cannot block people from viewing, commenting, or responding to posts if this is based on the user's viewpoint.[72]

Is it legal to display alternative religious holiday symbols?

You have the right to place alternative religious or non-religious symbols in a holiday display at a government building. This is a subset of the **public forum** issue. It explains why the government must allow displays by groups like atheists and Satanists. However, this does not extend to private property that is not owned or controlled by the government.

Unprotected Speech

What types of speech are not protected by the 1st amendment?

The government may restrict your right to:

- Yell "fire" in a crowded theater, or other speech that incites imminent lawless action.[73]
- Make **true threats** of violence against another person, where the speaker actually intends to carry out the threat.[74]

- Make **obscene** expression; this is a very high standard, and very few things are obscene enough to be prohibited.[75]
- As a student, make an obscene speech at a school-sponsored event.[76]
- Create, view, or possess child pornography.[77]
- Burn draft cards as an anti-war protest.[78] The cards are considered property of the U.S. government.
- Publish false advertising of a product or service. In general the government can regulate "commercial" or business-related speech more strictly than non-commercial speech.
- Publish or say false things that harm a person's reputation. This is called **defamation**.
- Publish or say things that violate a person's privacy rights.
- Publish work that is protected by copyright.
- "Leak" or disclose government information which you know because of your security clearance.[79]

Compelled Speech

When can the government force me to speak about something?

Sometimes the government can actually require you to speak, called **compelled speech**. If the government issues a **subpoena** for you to testify about something, you may be legally required to do so. However, you may be able to "plead the 5th" (5th amendment right to remain silent if you believe answering may implicate you in a crime). "Pleading the 5th" can protect you against having to provide such information even outside a court.[80]

Note to journalists: You may be entitled to **journalist's privilege** so that you wouldn't need to reveal your sources to the government. This is generally based on whether your state has a **shield law**. For more on this, go to the website of the Reporters Committee for Freedom of the Press at RCFP.org.

Free Speech & Private Actors (Non-Government)

Can employers restrict my free speech?

In some ways, yes. As discussed above, private employers are generally NOT subject to the 1st amendment (only the government is). But some state laws do protect employees from being fired for certain political activity. See our online Guide to the Law for Employees for more.

Can Twitter or Facebook or other websites restrict free speech?

Yes, they pretty much have free reign as to the content on their platforms. As discussed above, they are not subject to the 1st amendment, as the Constitution generally only applies to the government, not private companies or individuals. However, public officials using Twitter or Facebook (or any other social media platform) may not restrict others from seeing or commenting on their account.

Section 5: What are My Privacy Rights?

What is Considered an Invasion of Privacy?

Privacy law is about your physical space, personal data and information, and your identity. Most privacy laws are state-specific. That said, most states use the following general rules. The general standard is that you have privacy rights in situations where you have a **reasonable expectation of privacy**, such as in your home. Generally, there is not a reasonable expectation of privacy as to what you do in public (anywhere the public has access), but it does apply in private homes, hotels, offices, etc.

Newsworthy exception: Exceptions to most of the rights of privacy are when the subject is **newsworthy** or otherwise in the public interest.

Personal Space

You have a right to protection against unwarranted intrusion upon your physical and digital solitude and private affairs. This is sometimes called **intrusion on seclusion**.

If someone is in a place which you have legal possession, such as your home or office, without your permission, this may be considered an intrusion on your seclusion, as well as civil and/or criminal **trespassing**. You could have the trespasser arrested.

The government & your personal space

Also, as we discussed, you have the right to be free from "unreasonable" searches by the government/police of your body or anything you are wearing, your home, and some other personal areas.

Can people take pictures and video of me without my consent?

Although specific privacy and surveillance laws vary by state, again the general rule is whether or not you have a **reasonable expectation of privacy** in the location where you are being filmed. So, if you are in a public place, then most likely it's legal for other people to record you. If you are inside a private home, even an Airbnb, it is likely a violation and invasion of privacy if there are cameras recording you without your consent. But cameras on the outside of the house are generally legal.

Your Private Information & Data

It is generally illegal to intentionally publish embarrassing or personal information about someone when that information is not already known to the public. This is the law against **public disclosure of private facts**.

Any documents or information that is publicly available may be legally collected and published. However, many people don't realize that much information about them is in the **public record**. Some examples include most civil and criminal legal backgrounds, including lawsuits and criminal records (unless **sealed** by a court), and property information such as when someone bought their house and for how much money.

The government & your info

As discussed in the section regarding interacting with police, the police and government may be able to legally search and obtain certain information from you without your consent. Under the Patriot Act, the National Security Agency used to have the power to collect records in bulk, such as when the government required Verizon to turn over all of its millions of customers' phone **metadata** (metadata includes the number dialed, how long the call was, etc., but generally not the content of the call). But they can't do this anymore, under the USA Freedom Act.

Internet & your info

In general, most Americans don't currently have rights to data about your internet usage, or a **right to be forgotten**, unlike in Europe with the General Data Protection Regulation (GDPR). Any publicly available information about you can be posted on the internet, and you generally don't have a right to get it taken down. Other than that, your rights with respect to personal data collected by companies on the internet are generally determined by the relevant privacy policies posted by the company.

However, as of January 1, 2020, California consumers have many new rights of privacy and rights in their personal information. Under the California Consumer Privacy Act, companies must make it easy for consumers to opt out of the sale of their info, and delete the info the company has.

Do health care providers or other professionals have the right to share my medical information without my permission?

Generally, no. They must protect the privacy of your medical records.[81] The relevant law is called the Health Insurance Portability and Accountability Act (HIPAA). See more about health related issues at our online Guide to Healthcare Law.

Rights in Your Identity

Portrayal in false light

It is generally illegal to publish information that would make someone look worse than they really are. This is known as **portrayal in false light**. It is related to defamation, but in defamation the facts must be false. In portrayal in false light, the facts can be true but pieced together in such a way as to give a misleading impression of a person.

What is identity theft?

Identity theft is the illegal use of someone's identifying information for **fraudulent** (false and deceitful) purposes. It happens to just about everyone at some point. For example, many identity thieves open a credit card in someone else's name and use it to buy things for themselves.

Can someone post or share a photo or video of me without my consent?

If a person is legally allowed to *take* a photo or video, then generally they are allowed to post or share it. As above, it depends on whether you have a reasonable expectation of privacy in the location where you are being filmed. The main exception is that they can't make money from the image without your permission (see below).

Commercializing your identity

In general, you can't use another person's **likeness** for a commercial purpose (to make money) without their permission. This is known by a few different terms: **personality rights, right against appropriation of likeness,** and **right of publicity**.

You don't need to be famous to have publicity rights. Likeness generally includes a person's image, voice, name, signature, or anything else that would identify a particular person. For example, you can't take a photo of someone to use in an ad campaign unless the person agrees to **release** these rights (often for a price).

Mail, Email and other Communications

Is it illegal to read someone else's mail?

Yes, intentionally opening someone else's mail without their permission is a federal crime, which could subject you to a fine and/or up to 5 years in prison.[82]

Is it illegal to read someone else's email?

If you access an email account without their permission, whether because you got their password somehow, or you went on their computer, this is likely considered illegal hacking, under the Computer Fraud and Abuse Act; and/or invasion of privacy (intrusion on seclusion). A Michigan professor, who also happened to be a 7-time Jeopardy! champion, was convicted and sentenced to probation for accessing her colleagues' email accounts after the college reset passwords and assigned everyone the same temporary password.[83] Shame on her, but also, shame on the college IT department for that obvious misstep.

Section 6: What are My Rights in My Home?

Trespass & Disturbances

What are my rights if someone is in my home without my permission?

If you have legal possession of a property (you are the owner or tenant), a person who is on your property without your consent is likely committing a criminal and/or civil **trespass**. You have the right to remove them from the premises, and potentially press charges or sue for any harms this caused you.

What are my rights if someone is disturbing the use of my home?

If a neighbor or someone else is interfering with the enjoyment or use of your home on an ongoing basis, this may amount to an illegal **nuisance**. This applies whether you are an owner or tenant. Some examples include severe and ongoing things like noise, vibration, pollution, excessive light, etc. If you experience one or more of these, you may be able to successfully sue for nuisance.

Regulation of Property Ownership

Can the government tell me what I can and can't do with my property?

Yes, in particular, through zoning and land use laws, landlord-tenant laws, and the building code.[84]

Can the government seize my property for any reason?

The government generally may take private property for "public use," which has been interpreted quite broadly by the courts.[85] This governmental power is called **eminent domain**. However, the government must provide "just compensation" for such takings. In the 5th amendment of the U.S. Constitution, it says "private property [shall not] be taken for public use, without just compensation." Generally, the compensation required is **fair market value**.

One situation that outraged many was when the city of New London, Connecticut used its eminent domain power to attempt to revitalize the struggling town. As part of a plan to redevelop 90 acres of land, the city seized private property from homeowners against their will, although it paid them fair market value. The homeowners sued the city for violating the 5th amendment. But the U.S. Supreme Court ruled that the general benefits to the community from the potential economic growth met the definition of "public use."

People from across the political spectrum, conservatives and liberals, were upset about the decision. As a result, almost every state now has laws limiting the power of cities to use eminent domain for economic development.

It is also considered a **partial taking** of property when the government requires an owner to suffer a permanent physical invasion of the property, however minor. This also applies where the government authorizes a private third party to do so. For example, where the government tells a cable company they are allowed to place cables on private property despite the property owner's objection, the owner must be compensated for this.[86]

Can the government place significant regulations on my property?

Yes, but if the regulations completely deprive an owner of "all economically beneficial use" of the property, this is considered essentially the same as physically "taking" the property. The government would then be required to provide "just compensation."

Renters Rights

Renters, or **tenants**, may have significant rights or not many rights, depending on the state and city. Many large cities, including New York, Los Angeles, San Francisco, and Washington, D.C. have some form of **rent control**. This generally means that the landlord may not raise the rent more than a certain percentage each year (usually between 1-10%). Rent control laws usually apply only to older buildings, as restricting the income from property could discourage developers from building necessary new housing.

Throughout the country, there is the requirement that the rental meet certain minimum standards. Essentially, it must be **habitable** (livable). However, this can mean different things in different parts of the country. In most places, there must be working plumbing and electricity, and some type of heating.

Much of the rules for a tenant are set by the **lease**, which is a type of contract between the landlord and tenant (see below on contracts). For much more on renters rights, see the Law Soup website.

Section 7: What Do I Need to Know About Contracts?

Contracts come up in life much more than you may realize. In fact, just today alone you have probably agreed to several contracts, if you have been on the internet, or if you went to the store. Just about every website and app has Terms of Service and Privacy Policy agreements, which are contracts that you agree to abide by simply by using the service.

And every time you buy something, even a toothbrush, you are entering into a contract with the store. This contract usually says you agree to buy the toothbrush (usually you fulfill this obligation immediately), and the store agrees that the toothbrush will serve its expected purpose or you can return it for a refund. Your receipt is evidence of part of this contract.

What is a Contract?

A contract is simply an agreement between 2 or more parties that is enforceable in a court of law. This is not necessarily a formal document that says "Contract" or

"Agreement" or even a document at all. You can have a "verbal agreement" (technically called an **oral agreement**) simply by speaking with someone and agreeing to something. This may also be considered a contract.

However, contracts that are not at least written down in some form are much less likely to be enforced by a court. Even emails can be good evidence of a contract; although the most enforceable contracts are a formal document signed by all parties.

If you promise or pledge to do something, without another person also promising or pledging anything, this does *not* create a contract. To be legally enforceable, an agreement must be an exchange of some sort, where each of the parties "gives up" something. For example, when you agree to buy a car from someone, you are giving up some money, and the seller is giving up their car.

If only one of the parties agrees to do something, this is generally not enforceable. Let's say your friend promises she will give you her car when she buys a new one. She even signs a document with this promise. But you promised her nothing in return. If she changes her mind and doesn't give you the car, you're out of luck. You have no right to the car.

What is a "handshake deal"?

A handshake deal is basically the same as an **oral agreement** (aka **verbal agreement**), which may or may not be enforceable. Shaking hands does not necessarily make the agreement any more or less enforceable, but it could potentially help to show that both sides had a **meeting of the minds**.

Enforceability

Are all agreements enforceable in court?

No. As above, to be legally enforceable, an agreement must be an exchange of some sort. In addition, both parties must clearly have a "meeting of the minds" in that they both were generally on the same page about the deal.

Also, provisions or clauses in a contract can be unenforceable for other reasons. One such reason is that they violate certain laws. Remember that whole conflict of laws thing? For example, in some states, **non-compete agreements** (preventing former employees from working for a competitor) are generally illegal. So if a contract includes a non-compete provision, that provision is unenforceable in these states.

If I didn't sign anything, I'm off the hook, right?

No, that's not necessarily true. Contracts do not necessarily need to be signed, and don't even necessarily need to be in writing. It is *easier to enforce* in court if it is in writing and signed. But even if it's solely a verbal agreement, you may or may not still have a contract that you are legally required to follow. Again, check with a lawyer for your situation.

Getting Out

I signed a contract but now I changed my mind. What are my options?

There may be a **cooling-off** period by law that is applicable to your specific transaction. One such cooling-off right is the federal law that provides a 3-day period when you have the right to cancel certain contracts or sales. These include those made at your home, workplace or dormitory, or at a seller's temporary location, like a hotel or motel room, convention center, fairground or restaurant.

Whether or not there is a cooling-off period, there is always the possibility of cancelling or terminating any agreement or contract you enter into, at any time. But there is often a cost associated with this (sometimes a **termination fee** or **cancellation fee**.) Check your contract for this provision - it's often a section called "termination." If the contract says nothing about this then you will need to negotiate this with the other parties to the contract.

You may have a right to cancel or get out of a contract if one or more of the following applies:

- **Lies**: The other party **lied** about a substantial aspect of the transaction. This is legally known as **misrepresentation, fraud,** or **deceptive business practices**.

- **No True Consent:** You gave consent by **mistake** or under **extreme pressure**. The legal terms are **fraudulent inducement, undue influence**, and **duress**.
- **Extreme Unfairness:** The agreement is extremely unfair or one-sided, or the way they got you to sign the agreement was very unfair. This is legally known as the **unconscionability** doctrine.
- **Impossible:** The agreement falls through for some reason that was **not your fault**. This involves the doctrines of **impossibility** or **impracticability**.
- **Minors:** A person under 18 years old can simply cancel, void, or disaffirm any contract they sign, at their discretion.

One or more of these reasons may make the contract **voidable, rescindable, void**, or **null**, which are legal ways of saying the contract can be ripped up or unenforceable. If you are planning to rely on one or more of these reasons, you will generally need to have quite a strong case, and be able to prove your accusations.

In Breach

If one (or both) of the parties to a contract is not doing what they agreed to do, in a significant way, this is called a **breach of contract**. The non-breaching party must generally notify the other that they are considered in breach. If the breaching party then performs their obligation to reasonable satisfaction, the breach is **cured**, meaning there is no longer a breach. If not, a lawsuit may be necessary to enforce the contract.

Importantly, you must be able to prove your claims to the court. In the case of a handshake deal or oral agreement, you may need to prove that there was a binding agreement in the first place (unless the other party concedes this). This can be difficult unless you have witnesses or circumstantial evidence of some kind.

Article 4:
How Do I Exercise My Rights (and Fulfill My Duties)?

"The very essence of civil liberty certainly consists in the right of every individual to claim the protection of the laws, whenever he receives an injury. One of the first duties of government is to afford that protection."

- John Marshall, Supreme Court Justice

Article 4: How Do I Exercise My Rights (and Fulfill My Duties)?

Just about everyone needs legal help at some point. We all have problems, right? If you don't have any problems, well, there may be something wrong with you!

But seriously, legal issues come up from time to time, and they are not just related to bad times. You may want to start a business or nonprofit organization, or you may acquire some significant assets that you want to manage and protect. Whatever the reason, getting legal help should not be its own challenge. Whether you need help now or in the future, here's what you need to know.

Section 1: Options for Legal Help

I just have a quick legal question. What are my options?

First, check Law Soup's Legal Guides to see if there's an answer. (We're constantly working on adding more content. Check back often!) However, you should know that often a "simple question" is not so simple, and may require a significant effort to resolve. It's hard for a lay person to know whether your issue is fully resolved or not, which is why it's usually a good idea to check with a lawyer.

Or try attending a **legal clinic**. These are events where lawyers or law students are available to answer some quick questions and talk with you for a limited amount of time. They are usually free or cost a nominal fee, and you can find them at law schools or through community organizations.

Another great option is companies that provide lawyers on demand to answer your questions. Rocket Lawyer, which we partner with, provides a lawyer to answer your question within minutes, and for a small flat fee. See our website for more info on this great option: **Lawsoup.org/Rocket-lawyer**

You can also try posting a question on the "Ask a Lawyer" section of Avvo.com or Justia.com, to get answers from lawyers for free. While you may get useful information this way, these answers are often not comprehensive enough to fully resolve your inquiry.

I have many questions and/or need plenty of help... what should I do?

Depending on your legal needs, next steps for getting legal help may involve one or more of the following:

1. Hire a lawyer (or find a free or low-cost pro bono lawyer)
2. Contact an appropriate government agency
3. Find a non-lawyer legal help service, like an app or website

We will discuss these options in the next sections.

Who Can Help Me?

Your situation	Who to talk to
Victim of physical, mental, or emotional harm; damage to property; invasion of privacy; harassment	Personal injury lawyer; Police department/ District Attorney (DA)
Harmed by improper health care treatment	Medical malpractice lawyer
Physical or economic harm caused by a product or business	Consumer lawyer; Product liability lawyer; Environmental lawyer; Dept of Consumer Affairs
Harm caused by working conditions	Workers compensation lawyer
Violation of rights at work	Employment lawyer; Employment discrimination lawyer; Equal Employment Opportunity Commission
Mistreatment by the police or government	Civil rights lawyer; Constitutional rights lawyer; Department of Justice
Starting or maintaining a business	Business lawyer or corporate lawyer
Protecting creative work	Intellectual property (IP) lawyer
Protecting inventions	Patent lawyer
Marriage, divorce, child custody	Family law lawyer
Protecting and managing personal finances	Trust and estate lawyer; Estate planning lawyer; Financial planning professional
Immigration or citizenship	Immigration lawyer
Defense against criminal charges	Criminal defense lawyer
Problems with your apartment or landlord; or with a tenant	Landlord-tenant lawyer; Real estate lawyer
Problems with debt or need to collect a debt	Debtor-creditor lawyer; Bankruptcy lawyer; Collections lawyer
Tax controversies and disputes, including audits or collections issues; complex tax questions	CPA/Accountant; Tax lawyer; Enrolled Agent
Help preparing tax returns; tax questions	CPA/Accountant; bookkeeper
Help obtaining government benefits, such as disability payments, etc.	Disability lawyer; Government benefits lawyer

Section 2: How Do I Get and Work with a Lawyer?

To find a good lawyer who can help you, you can search Avvo.com, a directory of almost every lawyer in the country. Make sure to look for lawyers licensed in your state. Or try calling your local **bar association**, and ask for a **lawyer referral service**. FYI, a bar association has nothing to do with drinking, unfortunately; it's an organization that assists lawyers with their needs, and also often helps the public access these lawyers. You can find a listing of local bar associations through the American Bar Association, at Americanbar.org.

Be sure to check the lawyer's record on your state's **state bar** website. This generally provides information on when the lawyer became licensed to practice law, whether he or she is still licensed, and whether there have been any disciplinary actions against them.

Before reaching out to any lawyers, prepare yourself so you can save time and money. Write down your story, in brief, or in bullet points. Stick to the facts, and use the following questions as a guide:

- Why do you feel you need a lawyer?
- What specific harms did you suffer, if any? Economic, physical, mental, etc.

- What are your specific goals – do you want financial compensation? Do you want someone to stop doing something? Do you want to make sure your business is legally on the right path?

Just as with medical issues, don't hesitate to get a second (or third) opinion about your legal issue. Lawyers certainly don't always agree about how to approach a particular situation.

How do lawyers charge for their services?

Traditionally, lawyers charge by the hour, usually within the range of $200 to $1000 per hour. Whether a lawyer's legal fees are reasonable or not is a matter of the value you are receiving, and how the fees compare to what other lawyers charge.

Lawyers often require clients to make an upfront **retainer** payment, which is like a deposit that they will "spend down" as they work on your situation. The retainer amount is often $2,000 or more, depending on how much work the lawyer anticipates.

These hourly fees can add up quickly, and clients are often surprised at the tallies on an invoice. Fortunately, it is becoming more common for lawyers to charge alternative fee arrangements other than hourly. These include **flat fees** and **contingency fees**.

A flat fee means you just pay that total price regardless of how long a project takes. For example, a lawyer may charge a total of $2,000 to form a corporation for a client, and the client would then pay that $2,000 regardless of whether the lawyer spent 1 hour on it or 10 hours. This can be a benefit to both the lawyer and the client, as both have reasonable certainty about the total costs and there are less likely to be surprises.

And do you really care how long they spent on it? More important is the value they are providing you. If the $2,000 you spend on legal fees ends up saving you $100,000 or more by protecting your assets, that's a net gain of $98,000! Pretty good ROI.

It is not always possible to use flat fees for all services. If research on a legal issue is necessary, it can be very difficult to set a cost on this ahead of time. It could take 1 hour, or maybe 10 hours or more. In this case, you may want to discuss setting a cap on the amount of time the lawyer is authorized to spend (and bill) on the issue.

Contingency fees: If you are thinking about suing (or countersuing if someone is suing you), for certain types of cases, such as employment or personal injury, you may be able to get a lawyer to handle your case for *no* out of pocket cost. These lawyers often simply take a percentage (often 1/3) of any money you win in court. This is called working on **contingency**.

Lawyers may also charge for various costs related to the work, including printing and mailing costs, filing fees, etc. But some lawyers simply include some of these as part of their legal fees, or take the costs as a business expense without passing it on to the client.

All of this information should be contained in the **fee agreement** or **engagement agreement** that the lawyer will most likely ask you to sign. If you are not satisfied with how a lawyer charges, do not hire them and find a different one. If you have any fee disputes with a lawyer, contact your **state bar association**.

What are the tasks lawyers bill for?

Common tasks include performing legal research, writing memos and briefs – a legal memo or brief is an explanation of how the law applies or doesn't apply to the client's situation, writing emails, talking to the client on the phone or in person, talking to other people on behalf of the client, appearing in court, among other things. Some lawyers charge for every page they print, and every minute they talk to you. Others don't worry about the minor things. Ask the lawyer how and what they bill for.

I'm not sure I can afford a lawyer. What are my options?

If you don't have much income, you may qualify for **pro bono** legal services, which is free or low cost legal assistance. Unfortunately it is hard to qualify, and even if you do, there may not be enough resources available at any given time. You can find out your options for this at **ProBono.net**.

If you have moderate income, ask your local **bar association** if they have a sliding scale fee program, sometimes called **low bono**. Or simply tell them you are looking for a lower cost lawyer.

There are other options for certain types of issues. As discussed above, for certain types of cases, you may be able to get a lawyer for no upfront cost (contingency). For small businesses, the SBA (Small Business Administration) offers free consultations with lawyers for those who qualify. Also, low income criminal defendants are provided **public defenders** by the government for free, if the crime is serious enough.

The reality is that all these resources do not adequately address the significant legal needs of both lower-income and middle-income people. Our society should invest much more in helping everyone access essential legal services. Talk to your elected officials about this important issue of access to justice.

Section 3: Putting Government to Work
Exercising Agency with Agencies

On certain issues, particularly consumer-related, or employment/labor related, there are government agencies set up to help individuals with their situation. For example, if a business has not provided you with the goods or services as agreed, you can file a complaint with your local department of consumer affairs. If your employer is violating labor laws, you can reach out to the state or federal department of labor.

If you're not sure who to talk to, your elected federal or state representatives have **constituent services** offices that may be able to resolve your issue, or at least should be able to point you in the right direction.

Pressing Charges

If you or someone you know is a victim of a crime, or someone has threatened to harm you or otherwise commit a crime against you, you can take the following actions. But keep in mind that you may need to be proactive in exercising your rights as a victim, or a victim's family member.

You should maintain good records of the details of what happened, and (safely) collect and maintain any evidence of the crime, including communications such as phone records, emails, texts, etc.

Call 9-1-1, and/or go to your local police department to report the crime and press charges. You may also need to contact and follow up with your local chief prosecutor, sometimes called the **District Attorney** (abbreviated "D.A." or "DA"), or **State's Attorney** or **Commonwealth's Attorney**.

But ultimately the decision to prosecute is up to the prosecutor, not the victim. Because prosecutions take much time and money, if the prosecutor does not believe there is a good case against the perpetrator, the prosecutor will usually not pursue it.

You can find more local resources at the federal Office for Victims of Crimes: https://ovc.ojp.gov/

Section 4: Apps & DIY Legal

Are you considering using an app or going full DIY (do-it-yourself) with your legal issue? While I strongly recommend getting help from a licensed attorney, that's not always possible. If you still want to do it on your own, here's what you need to know.

Non-lawyer Legal Services

As an alternative to lawyers, new tech-enabled apps and other tools for legal help are emerging constantly. I fully support this type of innovation, as the traditional legal profession is not meeting the needs of many Americans. However, as many of these are new tools, and may not be properly tailored to your situation, they can potentially cause more trouble than they are worth. In my book *Do it Like a Boss*, I share a story about a client who used LegalZoom for his business, and as a result of receiving inadequate documentation for his needs, he ended up having to pay out

$30,000 to a partner which he would not have otherwise! You should only use non-lawyer legal services if you are aware of the risks and willing to accept them.

If you have a complaint or dispute as a consumer, **FairShake** can help you resolve it and get compensation. No cost for you unless you win money.

Need documents prepared? For personal legal documents like wills, or business-related services like LLCs, there are numerous options, including **Rocket Lawyer** and **LegalZoom**.

For help with certain civil cases like divorce, foreclosure, and debt collection, you can use **Courtroom5**. Also, for divorce help in certain states, there's **HelloDivorce.com**.

For the latest on non-lawyer legal services, as well as reviews, check LawSoup.org/get-legal-help/legal-apps.

DIY Legal Research

First, be sure to check the Legal Guides on the Law Soup website. If you don't find the answer in our Legal Guides, try reading a **treatise** on the topic. A treatise is an explanation and overview of a specific area of law, and usually a specific jurisdiction, such as Nevada family law. Some of the best treatises are called the "Restatements of the Law." For example, to see if you can get out of your phone contract, you can read the "Restatement of the Law, Consumer Contracts."

Treatises may lead you to the codes listed below. But, as you know, the courts have the final say on how the statutes, ordinances, and regulations are actually applied in specific cases, which is why you need to also look at the **case law**.

Federal, state and local codes

Codes are collections of laws passed by a body of lawmakers, such as Congress, the state legislature, and the city council.

Federal statutes are found in the U.S. Code, which you can find at **USCode.House.Gov**. State statutes are found in state codes. You can find these at the National Conference of State Legislators (**NCSL.org**), which compiles state by state laws on various topics.

Local laws and ordinances are generally found in **municipal codes** or **administrative codes**. Do a Google search for "[your city] + municipal code."

Federal rules and regulations

Rules and regulations are laws enacted by agencies within the executive branch at every level - federal, state, and local. These are created to implement and enforce laws already passed by the legislative branch.

You can find federal rules and regulations in the Code of Federal Regulations (CFR) at **ecfr.gov**.

Case law research

All of the above types of law are subject to decisions made by courts and judges. In addition, where there are no laws relevant to a particular case, courts and judges generally have to create law through their decision in the case (this is called **common law**). The decisions and opinions by courts and judges form the body of **case law**.

You can search for some federal and state case law for free via **Leagle.com** and **RavelLaw.com**.

Libraries

You may also find all the above resources at your local public law library, or possibly your general public library.

Article 5:
Where Do We Go from Here?

Article 5: Where Do We Go from Here?

What Do We Know?

People often say that they feel powerless in the system, so they don't even bother to engage. Certainly, there is an imbalance of power that unfairly favors certain people over others. But much of that power goes to those who simply have more knowledge of how the legal and government system works. And given that the vast majority of Americans don't even know the basics, there is clearly a large gap to fill.

Now that you have the basics down, this knowledge can be the basis for reclaiming your power. Let's have a look at what we've learned.

Humans have made great strides in treating everyone fairly, but we have much further to go. Too many people don't understand the basics of due process and rule of law. This leaves us vulnerable to a weakening of these vital principles.

Once again, rule of law is the idea that nobody is above the law, and the law is king. All individuals, companies, governments, and government officials are equally subject to the law and the Constitution. Due process means the government must provide and follow fair and impartial procedures when carrying out the law against someone, or when a person is even incidentally affected by the government's actions.

The most vital function of the courts is to ensure that rule of law and due process are upheld and maintained. They often do this by ruling against elected officials, which is why judicial independence is so important. Courts must remain as insulated from politics as possible in order to have the freedom to use their best legal judgment.

As we know, the courts are not the only ones checking and balancing things. Legislatures check executives, and vice versa. States and the federal government check each other. And the people check everyone (and are sometimes checked in return). It's the circle of life.

But this system doesn't always run perfectly. The structure could use some significant upgrades, particularly where the outcomes or potential outcomes clearly don't live up to our values (constitutional amendment process, Electoral College, etc.). And the system doesn't just function on its own. Each part must actively play its role. Our essential role is to get informed, to vote, and to express ourselves. Without this, the system will fail.

We have many legal rights, and many legal duties. Perhaps too many, actually. Too much law undermines rule of law. It is in part because of this undermined rule of law that many marginalized groups in society do not get the benefit of these rights in the same way as others.

"You have citizens who don't understand how government works and they're kind of soured on it. All they do is criticize. They have no idea that they can make things happen."

*- Sandra Day O'Connor,
Supreme Court Justice*

Towards a Stronger Civic Culture

We cannot rely on law alone in building a better society. Culture must begin to do more of the heavy lifting. For the most part, we already have strong rights against law enforcement overreach, and strong protections of freedom of speech. We have rights of protection from crime, from invasions of privacy, from violations of our rights as consumers and employees, and much more. These rights may have room to be expanded, but in general, more law is not the solution. We need a culture that truly affirms everyone as equal, and everyone as having dignity and thus *deserving* of these rights.

We also need a culture of responsibility among the people. Too many people are uninformed or misinformed, and not exercising critical thinking. Too many people are "checked out" and disengaged, saying things like "all politicians are equally bad." It's simply not true. There are many good politicians trying to do their best for the public. Yes, there's too many lobbyists and too much money in politics, but at the end of the day, you get to make up your own mind and cast your own ballot. And you can convince others to do the same. And you can even run for office.

Finally, as I mentioned earlier, quite possibly the most serious threat to the continuing existence of our republic is the recent efforts to subvert the votes of the people. While there have been various scandals related to elections throughout our history, the officials in charge of administering elections, whether on the Left or Right, have generally upheld the sanctity of the election process. However, certain forces, particularly on the Right, have been working to undermine the proper functioning of our elections. By lying about widespread voter fraud, some state and local elections officials are using this as a pretext to overturn the will of the voters, and assert that the votes do not count towards the chosen candidate for president or other offices.

While there are laws currently in place to protect the voting system from these actions, they must be strengthened. Fortunately, Congress is working on this very issue in reforming the Electoral Vote Act. Still, if officials intend to disregard and violate the laws anyway, strengthened laws will not be enough. Thus, we need to focus on rebuilding the norms of civic culture to uphold the system, regardless of who wins or loses.

What Are We Going to Do Now?

We know how it all works. We know our rights, we know how to exercise our rights, and how to make some changes. When enough of us have a basic understanding about the system and the issues, we can truly start to access our potential power.

Now that you know the basics of civics and law, what are you going to do with your new knowledge? As Marcus Aurelius said, "You can commit injustice by doing nothing." So, don't do nothing. Here's a few things you *could* do:

You can take bolder action in your own life because you know more about how to make things happen. Maybe now you have the confidence to start a business, or a nonprofit organization.

"The reasonable man adapts himself to the world; the unreasonable one persists in trying to adapt the world to himself. Therefore all progress depends on the unreasonable man."

– George Bernard Shaw

You can stand up for your rights and the rights of others by calling out when the law is being violated. Don't let the police bully you. And don't let criminals harass you.

You can work to change laws to make things better for society. Start local! Reach out to your city council. Or maybe even run for city council.

You can help change the culture by encouraging people to take pride in our system, and to participate in helping to make desperately needed improvements.

And you can pass on the knowledge to others. Strike up a conversation at a party, like "did you know that there are over 300,000 federal laws and regulations?" Or better yet, get some more copies of this book and hand them out to people.

Whatever you do, do it well. Thank you for your efforts.

"You can commit injustice by doing nothing."

– Marcus Aurelius

Acknowledgments

Thank you to everyone who helped make this book come to life, and who have otherwise made a positive impact on my life. Your help with editing, designing, feedback, and general love and support means everything to me.

Thank you to my family for sticking with me through my crazy ideas like starting a media company and writing books, and for your very helpful feedback. To my mom, Karen, for your enduring love and encouragement; to my dad, Davis, for teaching me how to write concisely; to my siblings Justin, Brittara, and Whitney, for your relentless optimism and positivity towards me; to their partners, Missy, Brad, and Matt, for your kindness and love.

Thank you to the amazing Jessica Chan, you are truly a goddess who can do *anything* and yet you still manage to be a humble and wonderful person; to the lovely Jackie Lam for inspiring me to pursue my goals, and for your editing help; to Dave Leon for saving my life multiple times; to Tim McNulty for your editing and humor; to Laura Jennings; Rafi Crohn; Isai Ramirez; Marko Budrovac, Akira Robinson, Kim Bode; Laurent Altier; Ruthie Tumambing; Roy Tumambing, Mika Yokota, Saewon Oh, and Tito Gonzalez.

Thank you to Deena and Terry of Green Pines Creative, for your generosity and efforts towards those less fortunate; and to all my clients for trusting me with your businesses and livelihoods. Finally, thank you to all my readers for your efforts to improve your life and the lives of others through the power of knowledge.

Legalese Translator: Glossary of Common Legal Terms

Administrative Code: An administrative code usually refers to local laws. In some cities, the administrative code is the collection of laws that apply to the citizens and other individuals within the city (e.g. New York Administrative Code). In other cities (e.g. Los Angeles), the administrative code is the collection of rules about how local government operates, while the *municipal code* (see below) refers to the more substantive local laws for everyone.

Affidavit: An affidavit is a written statement (sometimes a form) in which you declare certain facts to be true, such as "I live at 123 Main Street and I have known this person for 10 years" etc. The statement is made either **under oath** where a notary or other official asks you to swear or affirm that you are telling the truth, or the affidavit itself simply says you declare the facts to be true **under penalty of perjury**. Penalty of perjury means if you are later found to have lied in the statement, you could be charged with the crime of perjury.

Agency: Usually refers to an arm or sub-branch of the executive branch of government which carries out and enforces certain laws. There are federal, state and local agencies, for example, the U.S. Environmental Protection Agency, the California Coastal Commission, and the Los Angeles Department of Transportation, respectively.

Alternative Dispute Resolution (ADR): This includes certain methods of resolving disputes outside of the court system. It includes arbitration, mediation, and negotiation.

Arbitration: Arbitration is a form of **alternative dispute resolution**, meaning, an alternative to the court system. It is a private system, but is usually a legally binding way to resolve disputes. Many companies favor arbitration over the court system, as arbitration is generally much quicker and cheaper.

Cause of Action: A cause of action is a claim that someone violated a particular law. For example, if you have a contract with someone and they did not fulfill their obligations under the contract, you may have a cause of action for breach of contract. You could then bring a lawsuit based on that cause of action, as well as other potential causes of action, such as misrepresentation. You can sue for multiple causes of action at once.

Class Action: A **class action** is a lawsuit brought on behalf of multiple people (sometimes millions) with similar claims against the same defendant(s) (usually a company). It is an easier way to pursue everyone's rights versus if each person had to sue individually.

Clause: A part of a contract or law that generally refers to a specific requirement. It can consist of a few words or a few sentences.

Code: A code is a collection of current laws created by legislation in a particular location, including city, state or the country. For example, the laws passed by Congress and signed by the president are called the **United States Code**, sometimes simply **U.S.C.** The **New York Consolidated Laws** is the code of laws passed by the New York state legislature and signed by the governor. Local laws passed by a city or county are found in the local codes, sometimes called **municipal codes** or **administrative codes** or **code of ordinances**. Sometimes people casually say "the code" to refer to a specific body of law within a municipal or state code. For example, the Los Angeles Building Code is the collection of laws about building safety within the Los Angeles City Municipal Code. And often when someone says something is or isn't "up to code," it means it does or doesn't comply with the Building Code.

Common law: The body of laws that are created by judges in the decisions they make in cases.

Constitution: This is generally a document which sets out what the government can and can't do, how it functions, and what basic rights must be upheld. When people talk about the "Constitution" they are usually referring to the U.S. Constitution. But each state also has its own constitution. The U.S. Constitution is the supreme law of the United States, and no other laws nor government official may contradict it.

Contempt: When a court finds someone "in contempt of court," this generally means the person is disobeying the judge or a court order. The judge can then have the person arrested and put in jail.

Contract: Any agreement between two or more parties that is enforceable by a court of law.

Damages: In the legal system, damages refers to two things: (1) the harm a person has been caused by another, which may include monetary, physical, emotional or other types; and (2) the amount of money you claim you are owed due to the harms suffered (**money damages**).

Defendant: In a lawsuit or criminal proceeding, this is the person or entity being sued or prosecuted.

Deposition: A deposition is similar to testifying in court, except that it is done *outside* court, such as in a law office.

Domicile: A person's legally defined residency, usually where you live for more than 6 months of the year.

Due Process: The requirement that the government must respect the legal rights of all people. In particular, the government must uphold the due process of law and follow the proper procedures when enforcing the law against an individual, or when otherwise taking an action that could deprive a person of "life, liberty, or property." This comes from the U.S. Constitution, 5th and 14th Amendments. Related to the concept of Rule of Law.

Execute (an agreement): To execute an agreement or contract is simply to sign it.

Glossary

Executive Order: An executive order is an order by a president or governor to his or her administration (government agencies) regarding the way they are conducting their operations

Felony: Crimes are generally classified as either a misdemeanor (less serious crime) or felony (more serious crime). Felonies involve a punishment of 1 year or more of imprisonment.

Infraction: This is a classification of a law that is considered a "non-crime" and less serious than either a felony or misdemeanor. For example, some states consider possession of small amounts of marijuana to be simply an infraction.

Injunction: This is when a court orders someone to do or to refrain from doing something.

Jurisdiction: The concept of the government having power over a certain geographic area or even a particular person, for the purpose of enforcing or applying the law, or issuing a court judgment.

Jury Nullification: The controversial idea that a juror ultimately can ignore the law and decide how they want a case to be resolved based on what they think is right

Legislation: Laws passed by an elected body of legislators, including Congress, and state legislatures.

Litigation: The process of resolving disputes through the court system. This begins with the filing of a lawsuit, and can continue through a trial, and ultimately a judgment.

Mediation: A form of **alternative dispute resolution** (alternative to the court system) in which a neutral mediator attempts to get the parties to voluntarily agree to settle their claims.

Misdemeanor: Crimes are generally classified as either a misdemeanor (less serious crime) or felony (more serious crime). Misdemeanors generally involve a punishment of less than 1 year of imprisonment.

Money damages: See **damages**.

Municipality: A municipality or **municipal corporation** is generally a city that has the power to make laws and function as its own local government, such as Los Angeles, New York, Houston, Chicago, etc.

Notarize: To have a document notarized means to get a **notary public** to sign and (usually) stamp the document, acknowledging that they have witnessed the document being **executed** (signed) by the person or parties listed on the document. Often this involves checking identification of the individuals executing (signing) the document.

Ordinance: An ordinance is a local law enacted by a local government, such as a city or county.

Perjury: Perjury is the legal term for telling a lie while **under oath**. Under oath generally means either testifying in court, or in a deposition.

Plaintiff: This is a person who feels she/he has been harmed in some way and brings a lawsuit against the person(s) who allegedly caused the harm.

Regulation: This usually refers to a law enacted by an executive agency, such as the U.S. Environmental Protection Agency or the California Coastal Commission. Rules and regulations elaborate on law passed by the legislature. But sometimes it actually refers to laws passed by the legislature itself when they *regulate* or seek to modify behavior of individuals or organizations.

Rule: Mostly interchangeable with regulation (above).

Rule of Law: This is the principle that every individual, government official, company, or other entity is equally subject to the laws. No person is "above the law." See also Due Process.

Settlement: A settlement is when the parties in a lawsuit (or potential lawsuit) agree to settle, that is, to no longer pursue their legal claims, usually in exchange for a monetary amount or some other concession.

Statute: A statute is what most people think of as a "law." It is legislation passed by an elected body, such as Congress. (Note: Laws other than statutes include court decisions and rules & regulations.)

Statute of Limitations: The time limit for how long after a person's supposed violation of a law that the law can be enforced against that person. For example, if the statute of limitations on a crime is 5 years, then the government has 5 years to charge you with that crime, after which it can no longer take action against you (with some exceptions). Or if a person has violated a civil law causing you harm, and the law has a statute of limitations of 5 years, you have 5 years to sue that person. Most laws have an applicable statute of limitations.

Subpoena: A document compelling a person to testify on a particular issue, or to give over certain evidence.

Unincorporated area: A town or other location outside of an incorporated municipality.

Warrant: A police officer or other law enforcement usually needs to get a warrant in order to search you or your property, take your property, or to arrest you. This is usually required under the 4th amendment of the U.S. Constitution, but there are many exceptions. An officer obtains a warrant from a judge by convincing the judge that the officer will likely find evidence of a specific crime in searching you, or that you have indeed committed a crime.

Zoning: Zoning refers to local laws created by cities and counties to determine how particular areas of land can be used (aka **land use**). For example, the city may decide that certain areas are for residential uses, or commercial uses, or industrial uses, etc.

Symbols & Abbreviations

§ or Sec.: section (as in, section of code)

CFR: usually an abbreviation for Code of Federal Regulations, which is the compilation of regulations created by federal agencies

U.S.C. or USC = usually refers to the United States Code, which are the currently effective laws passed by Congress

© = the C in a circle symbol is used to give notice to others about copyright rights in a particular work

TM = trademark, the letters TM after a word, phrase, or logo usually signifies a claim to trademark rights which is

NOT registered, but is used to claim "common law" trademark rights

® = The R in a circle symbol is used to notify others of a trademark registered with the U.S. Patent & Trademark Office

Esq. = this usually signifies that someone is a licensed Attorney, and is used as "Jane Doe, Esq."

References

[1] In a Newsweek poll of 1,000 Americans in 2011, 70% of Americans couldn't correctly answer this question.

[2] In 2017, only 26% of survey respondents could correctly name all three branches of government. https://www.annenbergpublicpolicycenter.org/americans-are-poorly-informed-about-basic-constitutional-provisions/

[3] Graeber, David (2004). *Fragments of an Anarchist Anthropology*. Chicago: Prickly Paradigm Press. ISBN 0-9728196-4-9.

[4] Erdal, D.; Whiten, A. (1994). "On human egalitarianism: an evolutionary product of Machiavellian status escalation?". *Current Anthropology*. **35** (2): 175–183.

[5] Christian, David (2004). *Maps of Time*. University of California Press. p. 245. ISBN 978-0-520-24476-4.

[6] Daniel, Glyn (2003) [1968]. *The First Civilizations: The Archaeology of their Origins*. New York: Phoenix Press. xiii. ISBN 1-84212-500-1.

[7] Pew Research: https://www.pewresearch.org/fact-tank/2019/02/15/the-changing-face-of-congress/

[8] Warren, W. Lewis. (1991) King John. London: Methuen. ISBN 0-413-45520-3.

References

[9] 'The 1215 Magna Carta: Clause 39', ***The Magna Carta Project***, trans. H. Summerson et al.
[http://magnacartaresearch.org/read/magna_carta_1215/Clause_39 accessed 20 July 2019]

[10] "What Does "State Fragility" Mean?" The Fragile States Index powered by The Fund for Peace.
https://fragilestatesindex.org/frequently-asked-questions/what-does-state-fragility-mean/

[11] The Fragile States Index powered by The Fund for Peace:
https://fragilestatesindex.org/data/

[12] Husak, Douglas, Overcriminalization: The Limits of the Criminal Law.

[13] See note 12.

[14] Just Facts: As Many Americans Have Criminal Records as College Diplomas. Brennan Center for Justice. https://www.brennancenter.org/our-work/analysis-opinion/just-facts-many-americans-have-criminal-records-college-diplomas

[15] Carter, Stephen L. "Law Puts Us All in Same Danger as Eric Garner" December 4, 2014.
https://www.bloomberg.com/opinion/articles/2014-12-04/law-puts-us-all-in-same-danger-as-eric-garner; Somin, Ilya. "Why the rule of law suffers when we have too many laws." October 2, 2017.
https://www.washingtonpost.com/news/volokh-conspiracy/wp/2017/10/01/why-the-rule-of-law-suffers-when-we-have-too-many-laws/

[16] Schwartz, Barry, and Sharpe, Kenneth. Practical Wisdom: The Right Way to Do the Right Thing
https://www.ted.com/talks/barry_schwartz_on_our_loss_of_wisdom/

[17] Los Angeles Municipal Code Section 41.29.

[18] https://en.wikipedia.org/wiki/Hurdy-gurdy

[19] Union of Concerned Scientists:
https://www.ucsusa.org/global-warming/solutions/reduce-emissions/the-clean-air-act.html

[20] Centers for Disease Control: https://www.cdc.gov/nchs/data/hus/2017/017.pdf

[21] Alexander, Rick. February 9, 2017. "Liquid Investment; Lasting Value: First Publicly Traded Benefit Corporation Shows That Mainstream Investors Have Bought Into the New Paradigm — Literally" https://bthechange.com/liquid-investment-lasting-value-6a31d0b6e7b2#.ihyl9c35c

[22] Wartzman, Rick. August 19, 2019. "America's top CEOs say they are no longer putting shareholders before everyone else" https://www.fastcompany.com/90391743/top-ceo-group-business-roundtable-drops-shareholder-primacy

[23] Oxford English Dictionary: https://www.oxfordlearnersdictionaries.com/us/definition/english/filibuster_1#:~:text=Word%20Origin,led%20to%20the%20current%20meaning.

[24] Trump v Hawaii (2018): https://www.oyez.org/cases/2017/17-965

[25] Bannon, Alicia. "Choosing State Judges: A Plan for Reform." Brennan Center for Justice, 2018. https://www.brennancenter.org/sites/default/files/publications/2018_09_JudicialSelection.pdf

[26] See note 22.

[27] See note 22.

[28] Bannon, Alicia. "Rethinking Judicial Selection in State Courts." Brennan Center for Justice, 2016. https://www.brennancenter.org/publication/rethinking-judicial-selection-state-courts.

[29] Wickard v. Filburn (1942)

[30] Boyd, Ovid. REFERENDA AROUND THE WORLD: History and Status of Direct Democracy

[31] Initiative and Referendum Institute, University of Southern California: http://www.iandrinstitute.org/states.cfm

[32] Poll: 92 percent of gun owners support universal background checks: https://thehill.com/blogs/blog-briefing-

room/news/211321-poll-most-gun-owners-support-universal-background-checks/

[33] Schrad, Mark L. January 13, 2019. "Why Do We Blame Women For Prohibition?" https://www.politico.com/magazine/story/2019/01/13/prohibition-women-blame-history-223972

[34] Gideon v. Wainwright (1963)

[35] Baldwin v. New York (1970)

[36] Bostock v. Clayton County, Georgia, No. 17-1618 (S. Ct. June 15, 2020)

[37] Griswold v. Connecticut (1965)

[38] See DOJ Civil Rights Division memo of May 14, 2012

[39] Cruise-Gulyas vs. Minard (2019)

[40] U.S. Constitution, 1st Amendment; Cox v. Louisiana, 379 U.S. 536, 554 (1965); Frisby v. Schultz, 487 U.S. 474, 480 (1988)

[41] U.S. Constitution, 4th amendment. Also see Brinegar v. U.S. (1949)

[42] Katz v. U.S. (1967), Kyllo v U.S. (2001)

[43] California v. Greenwood (1988)

[44] Place v. U.S. (1983)

[45] U.S. v. Knotts (1983)

[46] see Katz v. U.S. (1967), Hester v. U.S. (1924), Oliver v. U.S. (1984), California v. Ciraolo (1986); Horton v. CA (1990)

[47] Warden v. Hayden (1967); Minnesota v. Olsen (1990); Brigham City v. Stuart (2006)

[48] Katz v. U.S. 1967), Kyllo v. U.S. (2001)

[49] Karo v. U.S. (1984)

[50] Jones v. U.S. (2012)

[51] Riley v. CA (2014); U.S. Const., 4th amendment; Federal district court ruling May 12, 2015

[52] Carpenter v. U.S. (2018)

[53] NY v. Belton (1981); AZ v. Gant (2009); Knowles v. Iowa (1998)

[54] City of Los Angeles v. Patel (2015)

[55] U.S. Const, 4th am. See U.S. v. Karo (1984)

[56] 8th amendment; applicable to the states via Timbs v. Indiana (2019)

[57] U.S. Const, 4th am.; See Payton v. NY (1980)

[58] based on the court case Terry v. Ohio (1968)

[59] Floyd v. City of New York (2013)

[60] for exceptions see for example, Chavez v. Martinez, 538 U.S. 760 (2003)

[61] Devenpeck v. Alford, 543 U.S. 146 (2004): "While it is assuredly good police practice to inform a person of the reason for his arrest at the time he is taken into custody, we have never held that to be constitutionally required."

[62] County of Riverside v. McLaughlin, 500 U.S. 44 (1991); See, e.g., Fed. R. Crim. Pro. 5.

[63] this would be a violation of the "habeas corpus" principle or "suspension clause" in the U.S. Constitution and the Judiciary Act of 1789, according to Immigration and Naturalization Service v. St. Cyr (2001); and Boumediene v. Bush (2008)

[64] 18 US Code 242; 42 US Code 1983

[65] Kisela v Hughes (2018)

[66] Tinker v. Des Moines, 393 U.S. 503 (1969)

[67] Cohen v. California, 403 U.S. 15 (1971)

[68] Texas v Johnson (1989)

[69] Chapter 1 of Title 4 of the United States Code

[70] West Virginia Board of Education v. Barnette, 319 U.S. 624 (1943)

[71] Cruise-Gulyas vs. Minard (2019)

[72] Knight First Amendment Institute v Trump (2018)

[73] Schenck v U.S. (1919)

[74] Watts v. United States (1969); Virginia v. Black (2003)

[75] Miller v. California (1973)

[76] Bethel School District #43 v. Fraser, 478 U.S. 675 (1986)

[77] New York v. Ferber, 458 U.S. 747 (1982)

References

[78] United States v. O'Brien, 391 U.S. 367 (1968)

[79] Espionage Act; 18 US Code Sec 798

[80] Miranda v. Arizona (1966)

[81] U.S. Code of Federal Regulations, Title 45, Sec. 164.508

[82] 18 USC 702

[83] "Michigan 'Jeopardy!' champ gets probation for sneaking into emails." Detroit Free Press: https://www.freep.com/story/news/local/michigan/2018/07/20/stephanie-jass-jeopardy-adrian-college/809384002/

[84] Euclid v. Ambler 272 U.S. 365 (1926)

[85] Kelo v. City of New London, 545 U.S. 469 (2005)

[86] Loretto v. Teleprompter Manhattan CATV Corp., 458 U.S. 419 (1982)

www.ingramcontent.com/pod-product-compliance
Lightning Source LLC
LaVergne TN
LVHW041808060526
838201LV00046B/1177